THE NEW ILLUSTRATED GUIDE TO THE
AMERICAN ECONOMY

SECOND EDITION

THE NEW ILLUSTRATED GUIDE TO THE

AMERICAN ECONOMY

BY HERBERT STEIN & MURRAY FOSS

THE AEI PRESS

Publisher for the American Enterprise Institute

Washington, D.C.

1995

Available in the United States from the AEI Press, c/o Publisher Resources Inc., 1224 Heil Quaker Blvd., P.O. Box 7001, La Vergne, TN 37086-7001. Distributed outside the United States by arrangement with Eurospan, 3 Henrietta Street, London WC2E 8LU England.

Library of Congress Cataloging-in-Publication Data
Stein, Herbert. 1916–
    The new illustrated guide to the American economy / by Herbert Stein and Murray Foss.
      p. cm.
    Rev. ed. of: An illustrated guide to the American economy. 1992.
    Includes bibliographical references (p.).
    ISBN 0-8447-3894-8 (alk. paper). —ISBN 0-8447-3895-6 (pbk.: alk. paper)
    1. United States—Economic conditions—1981– I. Foss, Murray F. II. Stein, Herbert, 1916– An illustrated guide to the American economy. III. Title.
HC106.8.S7414 1995
330.973'092—dc20   95-12728
                                                                                                 CIP

The AEI Press
Publisher for the American Enterprise Institute
1150 17th Street, N.W., Washington, D.C. 20036

Printed in the United States of America.

CONTENTS

PART ONE: A Rich Country

PART TWO: Uses of the National Output

PART THREE: Who Produces the National Output?

PART FOUR: Distribution of the National Income

PART FIVE: Productivity

PART EIGHT: Distribution of Income

PART NINE: Poverty

PART TEN: The Structure of the Economy

PART ELEVEN: Wealth and Debt

PART THIRTEEN: Government Expenditures, Taxes, and Deficits

PREFACE TO THE *NEW ILLUSTRATED GUIDE*

We produced *The Illustrated Guide to the American Economy* in 1992 in the belief that talk about the American economy suffered from a lack of information and that an attempt to present some of the basic facts would be helpful. The response to our original volume prompts us to believe that a revised and updated edition would be valuable.

We have added new material to this edition. One section (Part Fourteen), the importance of which was highlighted by the recent policy debate, extends the discussion of health issues. Another (Part Fifteen) takes up problems in measuring changes in the quality of life, such as shortcomings in our price indexes and the treatment of expenditures for pollution control and abatement. The discussion of capital in Part Five has been broadened to embrace government capital and infrastructure, natural resources, and research and development. The section concerning the structure of the economy (Part Ten) now discusses small business, multinational corporations, and trade unions. We have also expanded the material dealing with the distribution of income in the United States (Part Four).

The present edition brings the data up to or through the year 1994, where that is possible. In addition it incorporates a number of other changes. One of those is to follow the practice of the U.S. Department of Commerce in shifting from the gross national product (GNP) to the gross domestic product (GDP) as the basic measure of the national output. The difference is very small for the United States, but use of the GDP puts the U.S. accounts into line with the practice of other countries, where the difference is more significant.

We wish to thank the following people who have assisted in the production of the present volume: Darryl Anderson, Julie Bassett, Allyson Brown, Virginia Bryant, Jessica Clark, Robert Fleegler, Tayfun Gurler, Timothy Komosa, Dana Lane, Cheryl Weissman, and John Zahurancik. Also, we have been advised along the way by several of our colleagues at the American Enterprise Institute. The authors take joint responsibility for the final product.

INTRODUCTION TO THE FIRST EDITION

Presidents, cabinet members, congressmen, senators, TV pundits, editorial writers, leaders of business and labor, and taxpayers talk about the American economy. That is natural and good. Much of our lives centers on the economy. A great deal of this talk, though, proceeds in ignorance of basic facts about the American economy or, what is worse, makes assumptions about it that are not so—or at least are highly doubtful.

Listening to TV or reading the newspapers raises a long list of questions whose answers would be relevant to the national discussion but are commonly unknown, ignored, or misunderstood, such as:

- How rich is the American economy, compared with other times and other countries?
- How is the national income divided—between profits and labor compensation, for example—and what are the recent trends in that division?
- What do the American people spend their money on?
- Is America becoming a "service economy"?
- How serious have recessions been?
- What is happening to the relative earnings of women or blacks compared with white males?
- What is the extent of poverty in America?
- How heavy are American tax burdens today compared with earlier times and other countries?
- What have been the effects of budget deficits?
- What caused the large increase of the U.S. trade deficit?

This book was written in the belief that a certain number of basic facts about the economy, important to the continuing discussion, could be identified and presented in a readily understandable way. By "basic" facts we mean those that refer to the condition of the country as a whole, that affect and interest large numbers of people, and that throw some light on the subjects of most widespread concern.

The word *fact* is more difficult to define. What we mean by fact in this book is what can be measured, expressed in numbers, and presented in charts. We recognize that much about the American economy cannot be described in this way. After all, as Adam Smith said, the economy is governed by an "invisible hand," and if it is invisible, we cannot make a chart of it. The facts we present are the outcome of the behavior of hundreds of millions of individuals. To describe and explain the behavior of these individuals and the interactions among them is the subject matter of economics, political science, psychology, and other disciplines beyond the purview of this book, or of any other except in quite abstract terms. Other important aspects of the economy—freedom, variety, justice, the quality of life—can be presented here only marginally, if at all.

Still, the kinds of facts we present here are important: they say much about the conditions we live with and constantly discuss.

Measurement of economic conditions and changes is inherently difficult for many reasons. What we are interested in is real conditions and changes that affect real people, but we have no way of acquiring all the information we would want about all the people and no totally satisfactory way of adding it all up if we could get it.

The problem of measurement may be illustrated by reference to one of the most common pieces of economic information, the consumer price index (CPI). Consumers buy millions of different products (including services) in different places in the country and in different stores. So consumers pay millions of different prices. No one can collect all these prices. In fact, the CPI is based on a carefully drawn sample of all prices, running into the hundreds of thousands but certainly not all prices. Then we face the problem of adding all these prices together to get a single number for the month or year that can be compared with a single number for another month or year. We cannot simply say that every price counts equally—the price of an automobile to be added to the price of a (pound, ton?) of spinach. So we give each price a weight in proportion to how much "consumers" spend on the product.

But different consumers spend different amounts on different products. If the price of spinach goes up, that is not an increase in consumers' prices for someone who hates spinach and never buys it. We are necessarily forced to rely on averages that may not fit any one person very well. We also have a big problem in defining the "product" that is being priced. Products change in quality from one time to another, and it is hard to tell how much of the change in the price reflects a change in the price for the real value provided or a change in the real value provided.

Such difficulties bedevil much of the information we present here. But the statistical agencies that produce the data we use devote many resources and much talent to deal with these hazards as well as they can. Whatever their limitations, the results are superior to the casual and random observations that we would otherwise often have to rely on in thinking about the economy. But these inevitable difficulties are a warning against placing much weight on small and brief variations in the data. If the statistics show that the CPI rose at 10 percent a year during one decade and 5 percent in another we may rather confidently say that there was more inflation in one case than in the other. One could not be sure about the significance of a statistic showing 5 percent in one year and 6 percent in another.

In the pages that follow we have tried to confine the presentation to data of significant magnitude and durability. We have not made much of minutiae, and we have not made forecasts.

The selection and presentation of information here are as objective as we can make them. We have tried not to make a book of Republican or Democratic, conservative or liberal, optimistic or pessimistic data, and as we look at what has emerged we do not think the result is biased. We believe that most would agree that any reasonable description of the American economy would have to include much of the information we present here. Moreover, we have not sought exotic or iconoclastic data. We have not looked for things that would surprise the reader, although, despite the fact that both of us have spent about fifty years with statistics like these, some things did surprise us.

Most of the information presented here relates to the period since 1947. Not going back earlier was dictated partly by the availability of data but mainly by the belief that the Great Depression and World War II were a watershed, before which relevance falls off rapidly. In some cases, however, information is carried back to 1929 and in a few cases earlier than that. We have tried to carry the information through 1990, but that has not always been possible.

We relied heavily on the National Income and Product Accounts (NIPA), estimated regularly by the Bureau of Economic Analysis of the Department of Commerce. These accounts have the advantage of being a comprehensive statement of the sources, uses, and distribution of U.S. output that is internally consistent and conceptually uniform through time. These accounts yield the estimate of the gross national product (GNP), the most inclusive measurement of the performance of the

American economy we have. We devote many pages here to looking at the GNP in various ways.

Since we are generally interested in the behavior of the "real" economy, as distinguished from the "nominal" economy that reflects price changes, in many cases we use figures in "1982 dollars." That is, we are using estimates of what the value of output, purchases, and other variables would have been if everything had been valued at 1982 prices. We use 1982 because that was the year used by the Department of Commerce when this book was being written. The charts and data in this book are based on data available before September 1, 1991.

Around the time this book was published, the Commerce Department switched the base year for calculating real GNP from 1982 to 1987. This kind of change has been the practice of the Commerce Department over the decades; as time has passed, more up-to-date price indexes have been used to calculate real GNP. Every time this kind of shift occurs, however, the past may be rewritten to some extent. For example, the annual rate of change in real GNP from 1982 to 1990 is about one-quarter of 1 percent less when measured in 1987 prices than what it is when measured in 1982 prices. We found no simple way of getting around this problem. Some of the results presented here will look a little different with the newer statistics, but we do not believe that any of the broad conclusions about the economy in the post–World War II period would be seriously altered by the shift to the newer price indexes.

The Commerce Department has also switched from using gross national product as the most inclusive measure of the American economy, which we also use in this volume, to using gross domestic product (GDP). The difference is that GNP includes income earned by American labor and capital abroad and excludes income earned by foreign labor and capital here, while GDP does the reverse. In the postwar period GNP has usually exceeded GDP by less than 1 percent and never by more than 2 percent. This difference also does not significantly alter the statements made here about the U.S. economy.

We wish to thank the American Enterprise Institute and the Pew Charitable Trusts for financial assistance; Paula Duggan, with Michael Frank, for graphics, drafting, and layout; Laura Hardy, Jeffrey Liang, Mikel Morton, and Marc Shachtman for assistance with research and production; and Marvin Kosters, Mickey Levy, June O'Neill, Robert Parker, and

Carolyn Weaver for provision of information on a variety of subjects. The data used herein come, of course, from a large variety of sources to which we are totally indebted. None of the people who helped us is responsible for errors the book may contain. For each of the subjects covered here one or the other of us was primarily responsible for selecting the data, designing the charts, and writing the text, but we have joint responsibility for the final product.

THE NEW ILLUSTRATED GUIDE TO THE

AMERICAN ECONOMY

PART ONE

A Rich Country

Total output in the United States has increased greatly from generation to generation.

Total output and output per capita are the best available single measures of the performance of an economy. The total output of a country limits how much its population can consume, how much they can devote to investment to increase consumption in the future, and how much they can devote to defense of the country.

We use as a measure of total output in the accompanying charts the real gross national product (GNP). Real GNP of the United States is the sum of the total output of goods and services produced by American-owned resources, valued at the prices of a given year, in our case the prices of 1987. (In the remainder of this book total output usually refers to gross domestic product [GDP], which is the total output produced within our borders. The difference between GNP and GDP is small for the United States, although large for some other countries.)

National output consists of millions of different goods and services, and we have no completely satisfactory way of converting them to a common unit. In practice, different products are added together in proportion to their relative prices. With a few exceptions GNP as measured includes only output that is sold or bought in markets. Thus GNP leaves out some important items, notably unpaid work performed within the household. In addition, we must recognize that good data may not exist even for the things that are included. (Later in this book, we present recent estimates of some aspects of the national output that are not included in the GNP or GDP measures.)

While no great weight should be placed on the calculation, for example, that per capita GNP in 1994 was more than eight times as high as in 1869, no alternative measure and no direct observation would deny that there has been a great increase in output in the past century.

We must be cautious about interpreting the increase in output per capita as proof of a similar increase in "well-being" or "happiness." Whether people are better off with the higher output and incomes depends on what they do with them.

TOTAL REAL GROSS NATIONAL PRODUCT OF
THE UNITED STATES, 1869–1994

TRILLIONS OF $1987

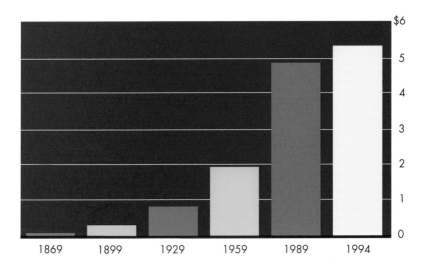

REAL GROSS NATIONAL PRODUCT PER PERSON OF
THE UNITED STATES, 1869–1994

THOUSANDS OF $1987

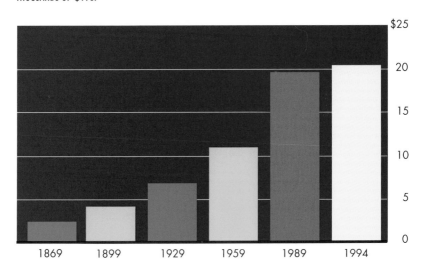

NOTE: The first five bars are spaced thirty years apart, but there are only five years between the last two bars.

Total output per person is significantly higher than in other large, "rich" countries—one-fifth higher than in Japan or Germany.

Precise comparison of the output in different countries is as difficult as precise comparison of the output in widely spaced years in the same country. Even if we know the value of the output of each country in its own currency, we have no precisely accurate way of telling what the relative value of the currencies is. In 1993, for example, the Japanese GDP was 469 trillion yen, whereas the U.S. GDP was $6.3 trillion. How many yen are equal to a dollar in the amount of goods and services they command? We cannot answer this question with certainty, because the Japanese and American products are different and the relative prices of the same products in Japan and America are different. The best, although not perfect, way to arrive at an answer is to calculate what the cost of an American shopping cart of goods would be in Japan in yen and in America in dollars. This gives one estimate of the relative value of the yen and the dollar. The same can be done for a Japanese shopping cart of goods, yielding another estimate of the relative values of yen and dollars. An average of these two figures gives a measurement of the purchasing power of the yen in dollars, allowing a translation of the Japanese GDP in yen into dollars.

The chart shown here is based on such calculations. The statement commonly heard that per capita income is higher in Japan or Germany than in the United States is based on much less reliable calculations, which translate yen, or deutsche marks, or other currencies into dollars at the current exchange rate. These exchange rates, however, do not reflect the purchasing power of the currencies in the full range of goods and services included in total output. Moreover, the exchange rates vary greatly from year to year, and calculations based on them bear no relation to the underlying trend of real output.

GROSS DOMESTIC PRODUCT PER PERSON
FOR SELECTED COUNTRIES, 1993

AS A PERCENTAGE OF U.S. PER PERSON GDP

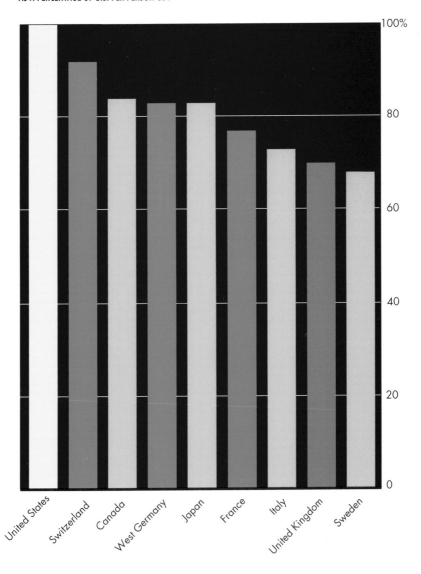

> **In this century all the countries that we now call advanced have grown at rates that are quite exceptional by comparison with longer periods of human history.**

During the twentieth century, per capita output in the United States and in other advanced countries has increased by about $1\frac{1}{2}$ to $2\frac{1}{2}$ percent per year. In a few periods in a few countries in the more distant past, per capita output may have grown as rapidly. For most of human history, though, the rates of growth must have been much lower, and there were some periods of decline.

One might suppose, for example, that in the first year of the Christian era per capita income in the most advanced place, presumably Rome, was about $1,000 a year, equal to that in Bangladesh today. If per capita output had increased from that level to the level in the United States today, about $20,000, that would have been an annual rate of increase of about fifteen-hundredths of 1 percent, compared with an annual rate of increase of 1.8 percent experienced in the United States in this century. That is to say, we and others in the industrial countries have been living in a period of unusually rapid economic growth.

Although, as the chart shows, the growth rate was lower during this century in the United States than in the other countries shown except for the United Kingdom, per capita output is higher in the United States today because it was already significantly higher in 1900.

GROWTH OF OUTPUT PER PERSON, ANNUAL RATE, 1900–1993

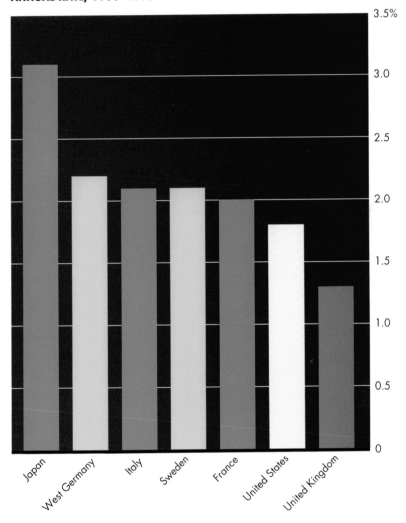

Most of the world's population lives in countries with output per person far below that of the United States, but the gap has been narrowing in some of the largest countries.

In 1992, 65 percent of the world's population lived in countries with per person gross domestic products less than 20 percent of that of the United States. This calculation is based on estimates of the World Bank, which attempt to measure and compare the real purchasing power of the currencies of the various countries. Of course, the difficulties already noted about making international comparisons of total or per capita output are especially severe when countries as different as the United States and Bangladesh are involved. If these calculations imply that a person in Bangladesh has an income equivalent to less than $3.00 a day, they do not mean that a person in Bangladesh lives as a person would live in the United States with an income of only $3.00 a day. But there is no doubt that the differences in per capita income are very large.

The concentration of population in the class with less than 20 percent of U.S. per capita output is heavily influenced by the presence there of China and India, which account for 40 percent of the world's population. But some other large countries—Bangladesh, Indonesia, Pakistan, the Philippines, and Thailand—are also in that category.

In some of the most populous countries, the distance behind the U.S. level of per capita output has been narrowing. The chart shows the growth rate of per capita output between 1980 and 1992 for the countries with population in excess of 100 million, except for Russia, where the data are not available. The growth rate of China is outstanding, but the rates for Indonesia and India are also impressive.

HOW GDP PER PERSON OF THE WORLD'S POPULATION COMPARES WITH U.S. GDP PER PERSON, 1992

% OF WORLD POPULATION

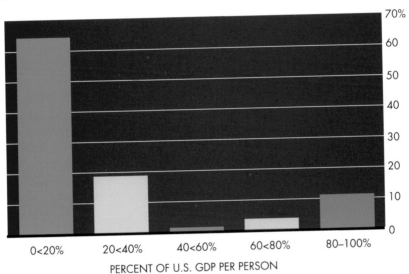

PERCENT OF U.S. GDP PER PERSON

GROWTH OF GDP PER PERSON, 1980–1992

ANNUAL RATE

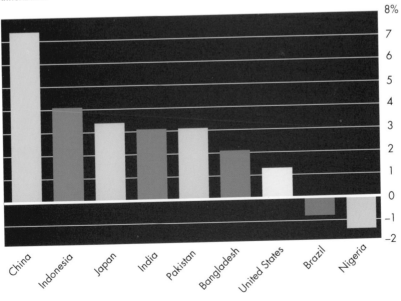

Even by the standards of American experience, the years from 1948 to 1973 saw exceptionally rapid growth in output per person.

In the seventy-nine–year period from 1869 to 1948, per capita growth of output in the United States averaged 1.7 percent a year, and it has averaged 1.4 percent since 1973. In the intervening years, however, from 1948 to 1973, the growth rate was 2.3 percent per year, about 30 percent higher than in the earlier period. Probably a number of factors contributed to the experience of that period: investment and technological opportunities left over from the depression of the 1930s and World War II, a great leap forward in the educational attainment of the work force, low and stable energy prices, a major opening of the United States to world trade, and the renewed feeling of confidence in the future as a result of having emerged successfully from the depression and the war.

The recent years seem divisible into two parts: one from 1973 to 1980, when the per capita growth rate was 1.1 percent, and one from 1980 to 1994, when the rate was 1.5 percent. One cannot yet tell whether the rise from 1.1 percent to 1.5 percent, which is an increase of about 35 percent, is durable or even portends further acceleration. The behavior of output per person is a product of the behavior of output per worker and of the number of workers in relation to the size of the population. Both these elements are discussed in later pages of this book.

GROWTH RATE OF U.S. REAL GNP
PER PERSON, 1869–1994

ANNUAL RATE

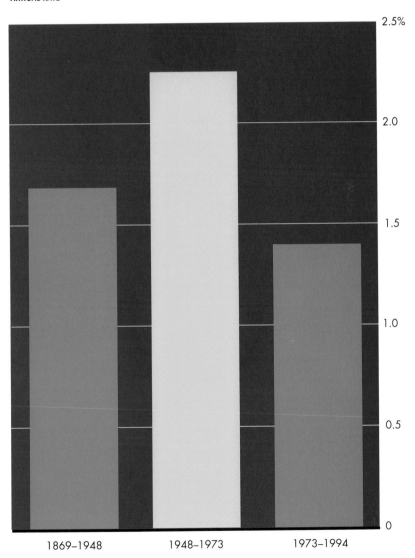

PART TWO
Uses of the National Output

Most of what we produce
as a nation goes for
personal consumption
expenditures.

There are different ways of measuring what we produce as a nation. The GDP measures production or output in terms of final demands: personal consumption, private investment, purchases by governments (federal, state, and local), and purchases by foreigners (exports).

In 1994, 67 percent of the total U.S. output went to personal consumption expenditures. About 18 percent represented private domestic investment: business outlays for machinery and equipment of all types; the construction of factories, stores, and office buildings as well as private homes and apartment houses; and additions to business inventories. Governments at all levels took 17 percent of the output, while exports constituted more than 12 percent.

The foregoing proportions add up to more than 100 percent of GDP. The difference is provided by imports. In the typical format for this country, imports are subtracted from exports to yield a "net exports" total. In 1994, with gross exports at 12 percent and gross imports at 14 percent, net exports were negative by about 2 percent. Showing imports and exports separately, as is done on the adjoining page, gives a clearer idea of the importance of all foreign trade in the U.S. economy.

SHARES OF REAL GDP BY FINAL DEMAND CATEGORY, 1994

% OF TOTAL GDP IN $1987

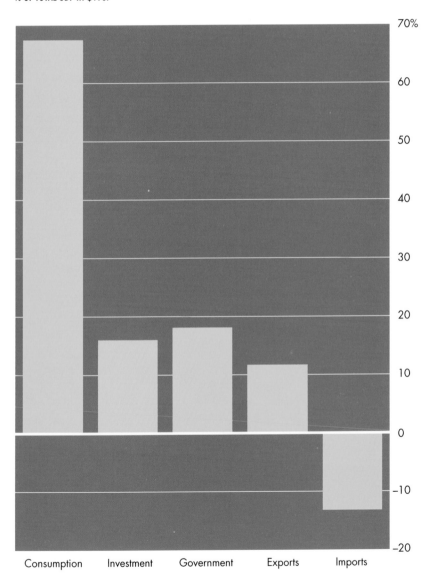

Consumption   Investment   Government   Exports   Imports

From 1950 to 1994, real consumption expenditures per person increased at an average rate of 2 percent a year.

What is meant here by personal consumption is the expenditures of individuals and households (that is, excluding governments and businesses) for their own use, except their purchases of houses. This concept differs substantially from other common-sense meanings of consumption.

On the one hand, it might be said that the entire output goes for personal consumption, either currently or in the future. Business investment, and government investment in things like roads, is intended to increase future consumption.

Government expenditures for national security are intended, among other objectives, to protect the present or future ability of the population to consume. Many other government expenditures provide services that are considered private consumption when paid for privately, like medical care and education.

On the other hand, some of the expenditures included in consumption have characteristics of investment—education, for example, which increases the ability to earn income in the future. Most consumer durables—automobiles, appliances, televisions, furniture—yield flows of services over long periods measured in years. From an economic point of view, it is only the value of such flows in each year that should be counted as personal consumption expenditures. In addition, some consumption expenditures could well be considered inputs in the production process—like the food that supplies the human energy without which work could not be done.

Yet when all this has been said, the measured total of consumption expenditures is the best indication we have of the extent to which the output of the economy is currently contributing to the satisfaction of the wants of millions of individuals and households.

CONSUMPTION EXPENDITURES PER PERSON, 1950–1994

$1987

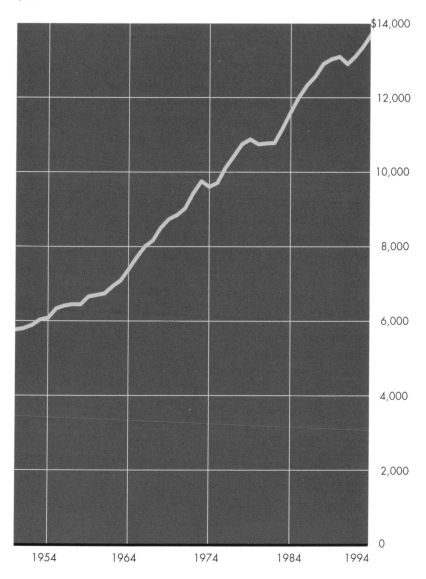

	$14,000
	12,000
	10,000
	8,000
	6,000
	4,000
	2,000
	0

1954   1964   1974   1984   1994

Since the 1950s, the personal consumption share of real GDP has risen, the private business investment share has been roughly stable, and the government share has declined.

Many factors are responsible for the rising share of personal consumption in GDP. Consumption depends partly on personal after-tax income, which has increased relative to real GDP since the end of World War II. The higher income reflects a rising share of labor compensation in income, an increased importance of transfer payments, and a decreased importance of personal income taxes from the early postwar period.

The rising importance of consumption in this country has not been unique. On the basis of data published by the Organization for Economic Cooperation and Development, from 1968–1972 to 1988–1992 the share of private consumption in GDP also rose in France, Germany, Italy, the United Kingdom, and Canada. Japan was the only country in which the consumption share declined.

Since the end of World War II, private domestic investment in the United States has absorbed from 13 to 18 percent of annual GDP, being lowest in recession years and highest during booms. But this short-run instability tends to even out over longer periods, as the chart demonstrates. Investigators who have analyzed data going back to the nineteenth century have found comparative stability—aside from business-cycle fluctuations—in the private saving share of GNP. As is pointed out further on, the saving share is the other side of the share of private investment in GNP.

The government share has decreased—that is, government purchases of goods and services rather than total government expenditures, which include transfer payments and interest. The share of federal defense purchases has been irregular but generally declining—to a level of less than 5 percent of GDP in 1994. Federal nondefense purchases have been fairly stable and relatively small, around 2 percent of the total, while the share of state and local government purchases has been generally rising.

The shares for both exports and imports increased, as will be discussed in more detail further on. In the 1950s exports and imports were about equal, but in the 1980s and so far in the 1990s the import share has been higher than the export share.

AVERAGE SHARES OF REAL GDP BY DECADE, 1950–1993

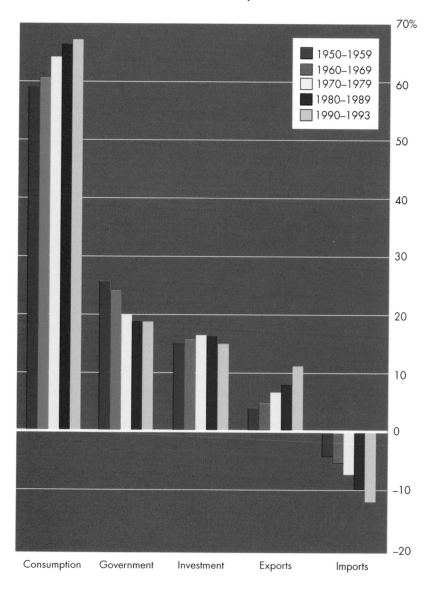

Legend:
- 1950–1959
- 1960–1969
- 1970–1979
- 1980–1989
- 1990–1993

Categories: Consumption, Government, Investment, Exports, Imports

Food and beverages are the single most important category of personal consumption expenditures. Their share of the total has declined, while the shares going to medical care and recreation have risen sharply.

The chart compares shares of expenditures on personal consumption in 1993 with those of 1963. The twelve categories embrace all personal consumption expenditures and reflect percentages based on 1987 dollars.

Over the thirty years, six categories have decreased in importance, and of these, only the category of food, beverages, and tobacco has decreased substantially. All the others have increased, although some have changed very little. The decline in the food share (including or excluding tobacco) illustrates one of the best-established laws of economics, namely, that as the income of families—or nations—increases, the proportion spent on food diminishes. The restaurant share of the grand total has also declined, but not as much as the share of food at home.

The rising share of medical care reflects higher incomes, more new but costly medical procedures and drugs, an aging population, and the increasing prevalence of medical insurance that weakens patients' incentives to economize on medical care. The recreation share (not counting what is already classified as transportation, food, and foreign travel) has almost doubled. Although about one-third of the rise reflects the huge growth of consumer electronics, including home computers, rising income and more leisure and retirement time have boosted other types of recreation expenditures as well.

These long-term comparisons should be used with care because they are subject to many qualifications. Although, for example, the importance of transportation expenditures has increased a little over the past thirty years, the statistics cannot measure the benefits of the greater mobility or privacy each individual has with an automobile at his disposal or of the time saved traveling, or, for that matter, the social costs of the pollution caused by widespread automobile use. Moreover, the figures themselves pose difficulties, several of which are discussed on page 246.

DISTRIBUTION OF CONSUMPTION EXPENDITURES, 1963 AND 1993

% OF TOTAL PERSONAL CONSUMPTION IN $1987

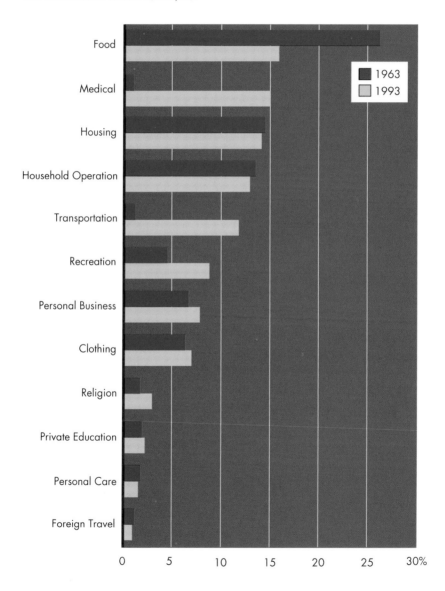

PART THREE

Who Produces the National Output?

Since the early 1950s the business sector has increased in importance, while the government sector has declined.

Consumers buy most of what the nation produces, but who produces the product? To answer this question, the Commerce Department distinguishes three sectors of the domestic economy: business, government, and private households and institutions. Under this classification the output of the government sector is measured by the pay of government civilian employees and that of members of the armed forces. The paper, pencils, computers, tanks, and missiles bought by government are produced in the business sector.

The three sectors are very unequal in size. In the American economy, most of what is produced is produced in the business sector, where ownership and operations are in private hands. In 1994 the business sector's share of GDP—at 86 percent—was little different from what it was in 1929, but many changes are evident within the sixty-four–year span. With the coming of the New Deal during the Great Depression and with the rapid growth of government payrolls, the business share declined in the 1930s and fell very sharply during World War II because of the huge expansion of the armed forces. Even so, that reduced wartime proportion (1944) reflected a level of business that was 50 percent greater than in 1929. Despite the many social and economic changes of the past half-century, the business share has gradually risen. The household sector, whose output is paid household work (cooking, housecleaning, nannies), was about 3 percent of GDP in 1929 but is less than two-tenths of 1 percent now. Nonprofit institutions—4 percent of the total in 1994—are a rapidly growing sector that embraces most private colleges and universities and not-for-profit hospitals.

SHARES OF REAL GDP BY PRODUCING SECTOR, 1929–1994

% OF TOTAL IN $1987

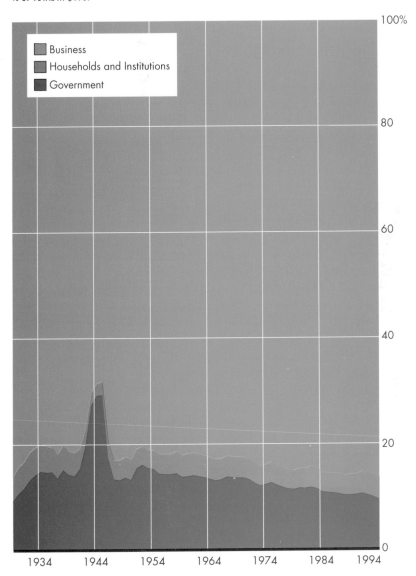

The service share of final demands has risen through the postwar period. The share of domestic production accounted for by service industries has risen more rapidly.

It is often said that America is becoming a service economy. That statement can be looked at from two different points of view: in terms of final demands for services and in terms of industries supplying services. In terms of final demands—that is, services in personal consumption, business investment, and government purchases—this country was well on the road toward being a service economy more than sixty years ago. In 1929 more than two-fifths of our real GDP represented final purchases of services. In 1994 this service share was 50 percent, as compared with 42 percent in 1948 (see top chart).

The statement can also be looked at in relation to the industries that provide services for the economy. The consumer who buys a refrigerator—a final demand—has acquired the output of many service industries: transportation, retailing, wholesaling, and real estate and finance, as well as those industries ordinarily referred to as service industries, such as advertising. In these terms, the number of broad industry divisions that supply goods—as distinct from services—is rather small: agriculture, forestry, and fisheries; mining; construction; and manufacturing. On this basis all other industries are classified as services.

Long-term statistics that show how much each industry has contributed to the nation's production—the supply aspect—are not available at this time. Using some old data for 1947–1977 and some revised data for 1977–1992, one can make these statements:

- The share of the nation's domestic private production accounted for by service-producing industries rose from about 60 percent in 1947 to about 70 percent in 1992 (see bottom chart). Since government is 100 percent services under this definition, including government would raise the current service share but dampen its increase over the forty-five years.
- The manufacturing share of private GDP was roughly unchanged from the late 1940s to the late 1970s. From that time to 1992 the manufacturing share declined, with much of the decrease attributable to primary metals and steel.
- Agriculture, mining, and construction all experienced smaller than average increases over the forty-five-year period. The construction statistics, however, are of relatively poor quality.

SHARES OF REAL TOTAL OUTPUT
BY TYPE OF PRODUCT, 1947–1993

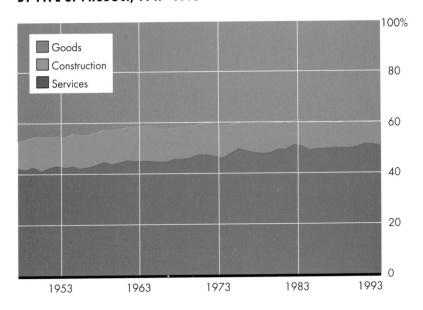

SHARES OF REAL TOTAL OUTPUT
BY PRODUCING INDUSTRIES, 1947–1992

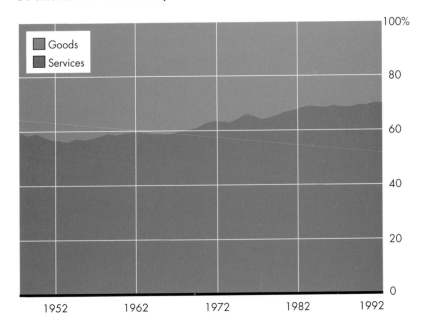

Few of the service industries are the traditionally low-paid, low-productivity personal and household services. But jobs with below-average pay are common in services.

There is a common perception that the exceptionally rapid growth of employment in services industries also means exceptionally rapid growth in low-paid industries. Some believe that the service industries consist mainly of domestic and personal service, where employment was, in fact, only 2 percent of the total industry employment, excluding government. Service industries, however, are a very diverse group that includes legal and financial services, health services, transportation, and public utilities. The average wage of all service workers in 1993 was about 96 percent of the average in all private industries. About 42 percent of all service workers were employed in industries whose average wage exceeded the national average, the highest being "security and commodity brokers and services" at $104,500.

At the same time, services, in contrast with goods-producing industries, embrace more industries in which pay is below the U.S. average of all jobs. Out of thirty-three service industries listed by the Commerce Department, fourteen paid below the average for all private industries in 1993. These fourteen accounted for 58 percent of private service employment and 42 percent of total private employment. An important part of the below-average group is retail trade, with pay only 61 percent of the average.

PERCENTAGE OF SERVICE INDUSTRY EMPLOYMENT BY WAGE LEVEL, 1993

% OF SERVICE INDUSTRY EMPLOYMENT

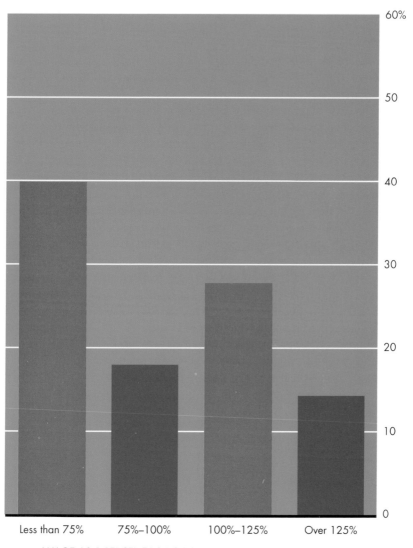

WAGE AS A PERCENTAGE OF ALL PRIVATE INDUSTRY AVERAGE

> Except during the depression years, the farm share of total output has declined in the twentieth century.

Over the past century, farm production has increased, but production in industry and in other parts of the economy has grown much faster. Today, farm business accounts for less than $1\frac{1}{2}$ percent of our GDP, whereas 100 years ago the proportion was about 23 percent. America was predominantly a farm economy in its early years; it was after the middle of the nineteenth century that industrialization made its most rapid gains.

Although growth in agricultural production was slow, it was accompanied by dramatic decreases in resources employed. The farm population was attracted by better-paying jobs in industry. Farm output kept rising because more capital, improved farming methods, greater use of fertilizer, better seed, and the like raised productivity. In 1910, when farm output was a much larger share of the total, the farm population was 35 percent of the U.S. population. Today's $1\frac{1}{2}$ percent is produced by a farm population that is less than 2 percent of the total population.

The farm experience observable in this country can be seen elsewhere in the industrialized world, except that in the past quarter-century the relative importance of farming has declined more sharply in other industrialized countries than in the United States. Today, agriculture contributes very little to GDP in the leading industrialized nations. The shift from farming to more productive activities explains a sizable fraction of total productivity gains. The United States realized these benefits earlier than the other countries, but farming is now such a limited activity in the industrialized world that the further gains from moving resources from farms into industry are very small.

FARM SECTOR'S SHARE OF GDP, 1910–1993

DECADE AVERAGES

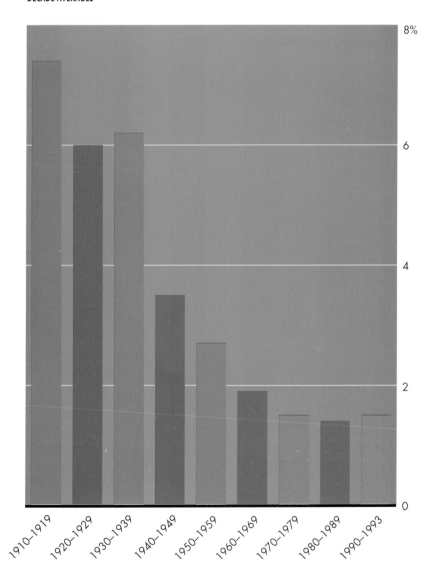

PART FOUR

Distribution of the National Income

Gross product is only one
way of measuring what
we produce as a nation.
Net product and national
income are valid
alternatives.

Most people are familiar with the gross measures of production, like GNP and now GDP, but in the opinion of many economists the net measures are superior. In this context the difference between "gross" and "net" is depreciation—capital used up in current production—and destruction of capital, by things like earthquakes and floods. One may ask why the value of current production should include the value of capital used up in that production if GDP is a value-added concept. There is a practical answer. Net product would be the most prominent measure of total production were it not for the fact that, in the absence of the necessary data years ago, it took the Commerce Department a long time to develop an appropriate set of depreciation figures. During that development period the gross measures became well established.

Another way of measuring the net value of output, just as valid, arrives at a total by adding up all the costs of production. That sum is the national income. The relevant costs are the earnings of the factors of production. The sum of these earnings—wages, salaries, fringe benefits, rents, and interest, as well as profits and losses—in principle yields the same total value measured in terms of final products, that is, by consumption, investment, government purchases, and exports, with certain qualifications. The value of products purchased in final markets includes depreciation plus excise and sales taxes, whereas the income shares do not. Income includes the value of government subsidies, however, which are not part of the value of products.

The chart shows in condensed form the relationship between gross national product and national income. For simplicity, the small adjustments that would show only domestic product and income are not illustrated.

Long-term growth rates are almost identical, whether output is measured from the product side or the income side. Differences show up over short time periods, partly because of differing data sources.

GROSS NATIONAL PRODUCT, NET NATIONAL PRODUCT, AND NATIONAL INCOME, 1993

TRILLIONS OF $

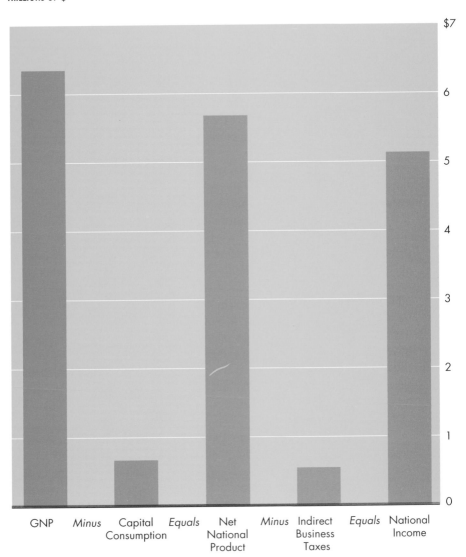

About three-quarters of the national income is compensation of employees. The share has risen over the long run but has not changed much since the 1970s.

The divisions of income observable in the national income statistics are determined by the availability of the data. The pie chart shows the distribution in 1994 according to the official national income accounts. The labor share (employee compensation) in that year was 73.4 percent of the national income, while corporate profits before taxes were 9.9 percent. The remainder went to proprietors' income, net interest, and rental income of persons.

From an economic point of view the classifications are not clean. The labor share, for example, includes what many economists consider to be a return on investment, that is, the investment made in the worker's education. Proprietors' income, which was 8.7 percent of the national income in 1994, in principle reflects what unincorporated businessmen earned as labor (wages and salaries) and what may have been left over—if anything—in the form of profits.

Other shares have their own peculiar problems. Corporate profits reflect the definitions of the Bureau of Economic Analysis; these involve several adjustments—inflation adjustments—to the so-called book profits that corporations report to their stockholders in financial reports. The adjusted figures are superior to the book figures for most purposes, but the adjustments are arbitrary to some extent. Net interest represents interest paid by businesses net of interest received. Unlike profits, the interest figures do not have an inflation adjustment, although many analysts think they should because the comparatively high interest rates of the 1980s, for example, contain an "inflation premium." Most of what is really rent appears as corporate profits because the owners of land are mainly corporations.

Over the past sixty years the employee compensation share of national income has risen dramatically.

If the compensation share has gone up, by definition the shares that represent property income—rental income, corporate profits, and net interest—have gone down. These are discussed in greater detail further on.

DISTRIBUTION OF NATIONAL INCOME, 1994

PERCENT

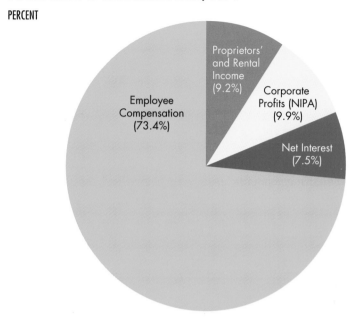

EMPLOYEE COMPENSATION AS PERCENTAGE OF NATIONAL INCOME, 1929–1994

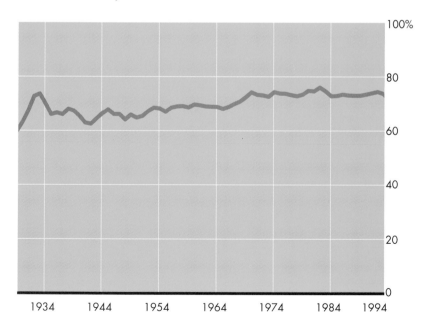

The fringe benefit share of
national income has risen,
while the wage and salary
share is about the same as
it was in 1929.

As a share of employee compensation, fringe benefits grew especially rapidly in the 1950s, 1960s, and 1970s and at a slower rate since then. In 1994, 18 cents out of every dollar of employee compensation represented fringes.

When compared with national income, as distinct from employee compensation, fringe benefits have risen from less than 1 percent in 1929 to more than 13 percent in 1994. The wage and salary portion of the national income has not changed much over the past sixty years. It was 59.6 percent in 1929 and 60.1 percent in 1994. In the 1950s, 1960s, and 1970s, the wage and salary share was a little more than 63 percent.

Fringe benefits, or contributions by employers, are of two types: those required by law—like social security and unemployment compensation—and those made by employers for private pension, health, and similar plans.

Benefits required by law—in the jargon, employer contributions for social insurance—rose rapidly in relation to national income after World War II as a result of higher tax rates and increases in covered wages under social security, new programs like Medicare in the mid-1960s, and expanded benefits to government employees, especially at the state and local level. Growth of this share of the national income leveled off in the early 1980s at about 6.3 percent and has not changed much since.

The other part of fringe benefits—private pension and benefit plans—grew even faster than mandated programs. In 1959 public and private programs were about equal in size, with each around 2.6 percent of national income. By 1993 the private component was close to 7 percent (middle chart).

In the early years pensions were the commonest type of private program, but they were soon surpassed by contributions for health (bottom chart). In fact, from 1969 to 1993 employer contributions for health on balance accounted for almost all the rise in contributions for private plans. In 1993 private contributions by employers for health were 4.6 percent of national income.

Recent research has shown that as income tax rates rise, employees prefer to obtain tax-free benefits from their employers rather than taxable wages and salaries, and to shift away from benefit plans in which the worker contributes toward noncontributory plans.

TOTAL EMPLOYEE COMPENSATION—WAGES, SALARIES, AND FRINGES—AS PERCENTAGE OF NATIONAL INCOME, 1929–1993

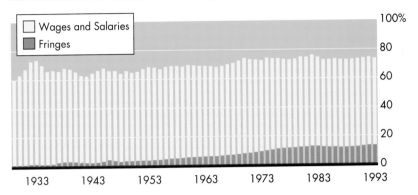

FRINGE BENEFITS AS PERCENTAGE OF NATIONAL INCOME BY TYPE, 1959–1993

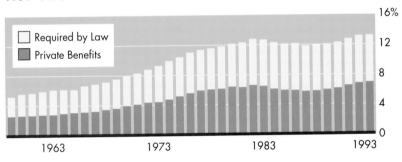

EMPLOYER CONTRIBUTIONS TO PRIVATE PENSIONS AND OTHER BENEFITS AS PERCENTAGE OF NATIONAL INCOME, 1959–1993

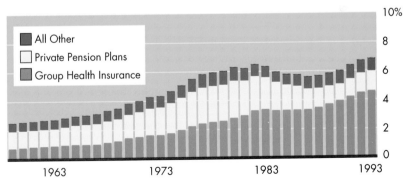

NOTE: "All Other" includes supplementary unemployment compensation, workers' compensation, and group life insurance.

The interest share grew the most rapidly in the post–World War II period.

In the national accounts, measurement of interest poses many difficulties that can be touched on only briefly here. Net interest in the national income refers only to the interest paid by business. It includes interest paid by individuals on their home mortgages and home improvements because homeowners in the national accounts are treated as businesses. Government interest is excluded on the theory that it does not arise from current production; it is viewed as a transfer payment.

The significance of the "net" in net interest is that interest received by business is subtracted from interest paid by business. Net interest in 1993 was $400 billion or 7.8 percent of the national income, but this was the difference between roughly $1½ trillion in interest paid and $1 trillion in interest received. Inflation affects both sides but not necessarily to the same extent. Interest rates peaked in the first half of the 1980s. The peak share (of national income) came later—1989—partly because it took some time before homeowners refinanced their mortgages and businessmen their outstanding debt.

A sizable part of the interest paid by business is imputed; that is, it is not monetary interest actually paid out. The imputation represents services provided by banks and similar institutions for which no charges are made since the financial institution has the use of the funds deposited. A bank, for example, may provide services to an individual who maintains a checking account, for which no charge is made.

Economists often view the interest rate as consisting of two main parts: an underlying "real" rate that would prevail in a noninflationary economy and an inflation premium that fluctuates with the expected rate of inflation. Some economists maintain that the interest share of the national income would not have risen so much if the inflation premium implicit in a nominal interest rate were removed from the calculation of net interest. Calculating that adjustment poses difficulties, however, mainly because the expected rate of inflation—unlike the actual rate—cannot be observed. Even so, there can be little doubt that the high rates of interest from about 1976 to 1984 reflected high expected rates of inflation.

NET INTEREST AS A PERCENTAGE OF NATIONAL INCOME, 1929–1994

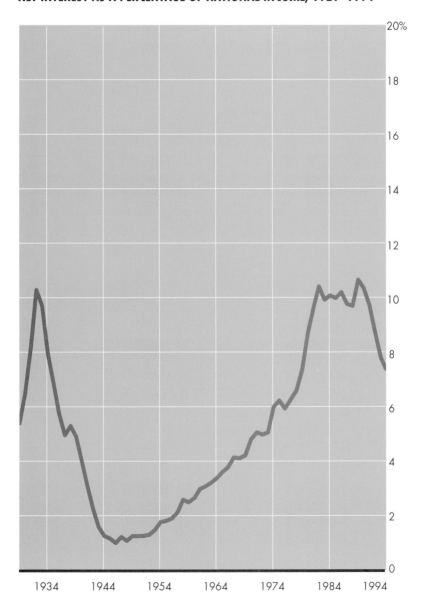

One reason for the rise in the interest share of the national income is that in relative terms business is using much more debt than it used to, as is shown on the facing page. Here we show how the ratio of credit market debt to national income has risen since the end of World War II. Credit market debt, on which interest is normally paid, excludes liabilities like income taxes payable and trade payables.

Economists do not have a full understanding of the increased share, which continued through the 1980s after interest rates plummeted earlier in the decade. Part of the answer is found in innovations in the financial field like the appearance of various kinds of "hedging devices"—options, futures, and the like—which provide protection against interest rate changes and have encouraged greater use of debt. Leveraged buyouts, so prominent in the 1980s, increased the volume of debt in relation to income.

The second chart, showing the yield on a U.S. Treasury note with a constant ten-year maturity, illustrates the rise in interest rates. (The pattern is quite similar to the pattern of a high-grade corporate bond on an annual basis. It is not greatly different from yields on three-month Treasury bills, which show greater fluctuation but the same broad outline over the period.) This particular series peaked in 1982 and traced an irregular decline through 1993. The 1994 rise is not illustrated.

The other line in the second chart illustrates the ratio of gross interest paid by nonfinancial corporations to the credit market debt of those corporations. This ratio is an average interest rate that reflects not only the rates at which business borrowed but also the changing mixture of debt maturities. The interesting point about this second line is how its broad contours resemble the "pure" interest rate illustrated by the Treasury note. One possible explanation for the similarity is that the mixture of corporate debt and the relative spreads among different maturities of debt have not changed radically. The overhang of existing debt that is not refinanced tends to dampen the fall in the ratio of interest to outstanding debt.

RATIO OF CREDIT MARKET DEBT TO NATIONAL INCOME, 1945–1993

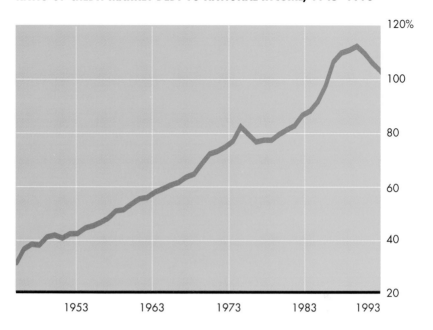

RATIO OF INTEREST PAID TO DEBT, NONFINANCIAL CORPORATIONS, 1953–1993

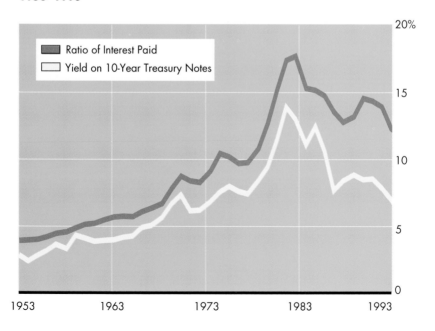

Because corporate profits are highly sensitive to changing business conditions, the share of profits in national income undergoes pronounced changes over the course of the business cycle. Although employment drops when sales and orders fall, wage rates are rarely cut. Overhead, much of which is payroll, changes only slowly. Businesses thus find their profit margins squeezed. In contrast, profits tend to rise very rapidly in the early stages of a recovery, because costs change very little while sales are rising.

Although the chart focuses on annual rather than quarterly data—which would be more suitable for analyzing profit behavior over the business cycle—it does appear that the profit share did not fall as much in the 1990–1991 recession as it did in the 1981–1982 recession. This is probably related to the severe cost-cutting measures that corporations undertook in the late 1980s and early 1990s. Profits as a share of national income in 1993—the national income and product accounts version—were the highest since 1978–1979; the share rose further in 1994.

The cyclical variability of profits is a well-known phenomenon, but less well known—or understood—is the declining share of profits over the postwar years. The greater reliance on debt to finance corporate investments does not explain this decline, because the combined shares of profits and interest also declined over the long run. One plausible explanation is that demand was exceptionally strong in the early postwar years because demand was so weak during the depression and supplies of things like houses and appliances were so limited during World War II. In this view, the less buoyant demand that followed the early postwar period was accompanied by shrinking profit margins. Perhaps more important, though, has been the intensification of foreign competition, which was largely absent in this country during the first two decades after the end of World War II and which has forced domestic producers to cut margins and costs to maintain market shares.

CORPORATE PROFITS BEFORE AND AFTER TAXES
AS PERCENTAGES OF NATIONAL INCOME, 1929–1994

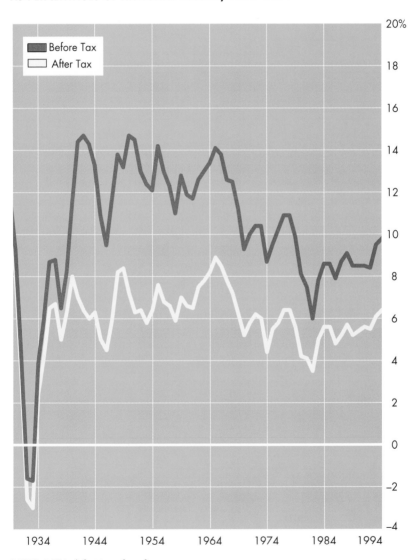

NOTE: NIPA definition of profits.

Stockholder reports of profits can be misleading. During inflationary periods they may understate the cost of goods sold or depreciation. The national income version of profits adjusts for these and other distortions.

When prices are rising, the profits that appear in reports to stock-holders ("book profits") will be overstated if companies use conventional accounting methods. Under these methods the costs of goods sold that appear on the books do not fully reflect the costs at which the goods were acquired, and as a consequence reported profits are too high. Companies, it should be noted, pay taxes on these overstated profits. As the rate of inflation rose in the 1970s, companies turned increasingly to accounting methods that gave a truer picture of their profits. In measuring profits for national income purposes, however, the Commerce Department has always made an "inventory valuation adjustment" to remove this inflationary distortion.

A problem caused by inflation also arises in the calculation of depreciation. Companies typically carry on their books assets like plant and equipment at historical cost and figure depreciation on the basis of these costs. But when prices rise, the depreciation calculated at the lower price will fall short of the amount needed to replace, say, an old machine with a new one. As an element of cost, depreciation so measured is too low, and as a result reported profits are too high. The Commerce Department makes an adjustment for this distortion also, the so-called capital consumption adjustment. Finally, changing IRS regulations regarding how depreciation is determined have introduced further distortions. The Commerce Department calculates depreciation on a standard basis so that this distortion will not affect profits for national income purposes.

The chart shows the two versions of profits. In the period of high inflation—from the early 1970s to the early 1980s—book profits were consistently overstated relative to National Income and Product Accounts (NIPA) profits because book profits included inventory profits and reflected abnormally low depreciation charges. Since 1983, book profits have been understated relative to national income profits, partly because inventory profits declined but mainly because depreciation allowances were liberalized under the tax laws.

THE NIPA AND THE STOCKHOLDER VERSIONS OF PROFITS
AS PERCENTAGES OF NATIONAL INCOME, 1970–1994

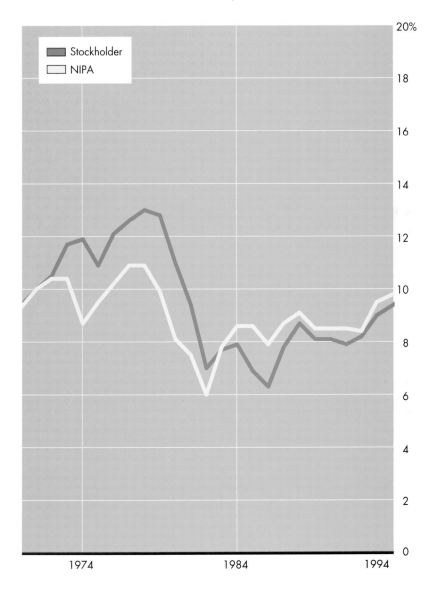

PART FIVE
Productivity

Over the long run, the increase in real output has exceeded the increase in the input of labor or the combined increase in the inputs of labor and capital. Output per unit of input is called productivity.

In 1994, America's real gross domestic product was about four times its level in 1948. What was the source of the production increase? To what extent did it reflect an expansion in the factors of production or inputs—the number of persons employed and the amount of capital they had to work with—and to what extent did it reflect increased productivity or efficiency of these factors? We are especially interested in measuring productivity growth because rising productivity is what underlies rising living standards and most of what we think of as economic progress. If the rise in productivity slows down, so will the rise in living standards.

The top chart shows the basic facts about the growth of output and inputs in the private business sector from 1948 to 1992. Typically, the growth of output is compared with the growth of labor input, which in simplest terms is measured by changes in employment and in hours worked per year. From 1948 to 1992, business output grew about 325 percent, or at an annual rate of 3.3 percent. Despite some decline in average hours, strong increases in employment (including the self-employed) brought about an average annual rise in labor input of 0.9 percent. This suggests a productivity rise of 2.4 percent a year (3.3–0.9).

This particular measure, while useful, fails to make allowance for the contributions of other factors of production available to the worker in the form of plant, equipment, inventories, and land. A more comprehensive input measure takes account of these other factors as well. Labor and capital are weighted together by the shares of income produced, and since labor gets most of the national income, its weight is much greater than the weight for capital. Over the postwar years, combined capital and labor inputs grew more than labor inputs alone—that is, labor had increasing amounts of capital to work with. But the combined inputs also grew less than output—2.0 percent a year versus 3.3 percent for output. On this more comprehensive basis, total factor or multifactor productivity grew at an annual rate of 1.3 percent. Clearly it has been an important component of the growth in output.

The bottom chart makes explicit the advances in productivity suggested by the chart on top.

TOTAL OUTPUT, COMBINED INPUTS, AND LABOR INPUT
FOR PRIVATE BUSINESS, 1948–1992

INDEXES: 1948=100

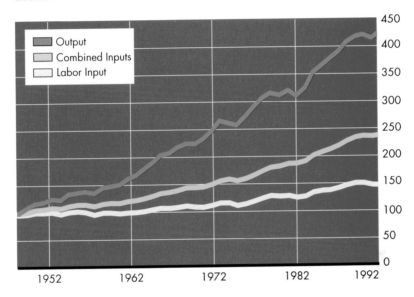

TWO MEASURES OF PRODUCTIVITY
FOR PRIVATE BUSINESS, 1948–1992

INDEXES: 1948=100

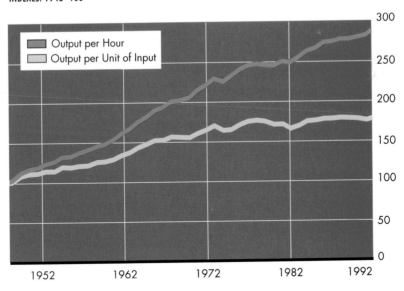

Part of the increase in output per worker is the result of the increase in the educational attainment of the labor force.

The increased education of the labor force has been an important source of growth in output since at least the early part of the century. Educational attainment and earnings go hand in hand. Some investigators like to view this rise in education as more labor input. Other investigators, though, measuring labor input solely by employment and hours worked per year, count the rise in education as part of productivity growth.

Education brings to the individual more besides skills and knowledge. The more education a person has, the more different jobs he can perform, the better he will perform, and the more aware he will be of other job opportunities. As recently as 1969, 38 percent of the civilian labor force between the ages of twenty-five and sixty-four had not obtained a high school diploma. By 1993 that proportion had fallen to 11 percent. In 1969, 14 percent of the same labor force had either a college degree or graduate education; by 1993 that proportion was up to 27 percent. Shifts in the educational attainment of the labor force are shown in the top chart.

A more educated population not only strengthens the society but also makes it capable of producing and earning more. The chart, which is based on figures for 1992, shows how income of men twenty-five years of age or older with year-round full-time jobs varied with educational attainment. A man with a high school diploma earned 86 percent more than a man with only an eighth-grade education or less and 43 percent more than a man with some high school but no diploma. A man with four years of college earned 61 percent more than a man with four years of high school. The story looks roughly the same when the focus shifts to women.

On the basis of an analysis made by the Bureau of Labor Statistics, it appears that the increased educational attainment of the entire labor force between 1948 and 1990 would account for about one-sixth of the rise in output per hour in the private business sector over the same period.

PERCENTAGE OF CIVILIAN LABOR FORCE AGED TWENTY-FIVE TO SIXTY-FIVE YEARS, BY EDUCATIONAL ATTAINMENT, 1969–1993

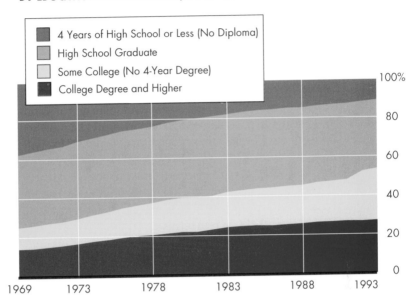

4 Years of High School or Less (No Diploma)
High School Graduate
Some College (No 4-Year Degree)
College Degree and Higher

100%
80
60
40
20
0

1969   1973   1978   1983   1988   1993

MEDIAN INCOMES OF MEN BY EDUCATIONAL ATTAINMENT, YEAR-ROUND FULL-TIME WORKERS, TWENTY-FIVE YEARS OR OLDER, 1992

INDEX: FOUR YEARS OF HIGH SCHOOL=100

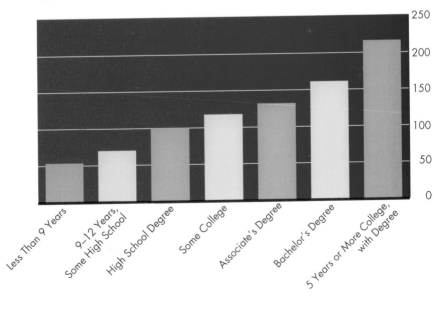

250
200
150
100
50
0

Less Than 9 Years
9–12 Years, Some High School
High School Degree
Some College
Associate's Degree
Bachelor's Degree
5 Years or More College, with Degree

Increased capital per labor hour has been an important source of rising labor productivity. All types of tangible capital have increased.

Capital can be viewed in many different ways. Most economists who have analyzed sources of growth have taken a conventional view of capital inputs as consisting of the services from structures, equipment, inventories, and land owned by private business. In the U.S. accounts, government capital is excluded. Most investigators also exclude intangible capital like human capital, which reflects the education, experience, and training an individual brings to and acquires on the job. The top chart, incorporating data from the Bureau of Labor Statistics, shows how private capital and its components have increased since 1948, in real terms.

The contribution an input makes to the growth of output depends on two things: how much the input has grown and the importance or weight of the input. Input weights are commonly based on shares in the national income (produced by private business) received by the inputs.

The bottom chart shows that capital services per hour of labor worked in the private business sector rose 247 percent between 1948 and 1992, or at an annual rate of 2.9 percent (compounded annually). In this particular calculation, "labor" includes not only hours worked by employees but also those worked by proprietors and unpaid family workers in private business. Capital has a weight of about 30 percent; that is, employees (including proprietors) receive about 70 percent of the income produced in the private business sector. The capital weight times the increase in capital per worker gives a contribution of tangible capital of 0.9 percent per year. Output per hour of all persons rose at an annual rate of 2.5 percent per year, so that the increased capital intensity of production accounted for 36 percent of the rise in labor productivity.

Some economists question the appropriateness of using shares of national income to weight the factor inputs. In this view, the market has many imperfections, as a result of which labor receives some of the income that might accrue to capital in markets with fewer imperfections. Small changes in weight, however, would not alter by very much the results just cited. Tangible capital makes an important contribution, but it is not the whole explanation of the growth in labor productivity.

PRODUCTIVE CAPITAL STOCK, PRIVATE BUSINESS, 1948–1992

TRILLIONS OF $1987

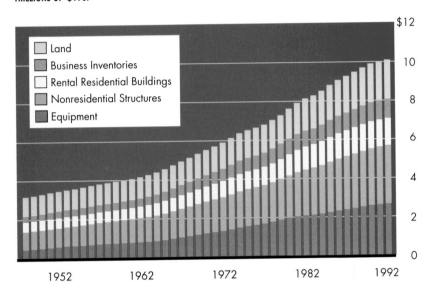

Legend:
- Land
- Business Inventories
- Rental Residential Buildings
- Nonresidential Structures
- Equipment

PRIVATE BUSINESS CAPITAL PER LABOR HOUR, 1948–1992

INDEX: 1948 =100

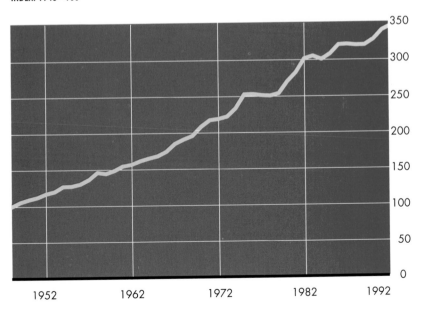

Private capital owned by business is only part of the nation's capital stock.

Governments at all levels hold substantial stocks of capital in the form of school buildings, dams, and superhighways, as well as trucks, computers, and filing cabinets. In addition, consumers hold large stocks of durable assets such as automobiles, household appliances, furniture, boats, bicycles, and consumer electronics. This so-called reproducible capital excludes land and mineral rights.

The chart plots net stocks of fixed reproducible capital held by private business, governments, and consumers, measured in constant dollars. Inventories held by business ($1 trillion in 1987 prices) and government should be included but are excluded here. The grand total of fixed capital at the end of 1993 was more than $14 trillion in 1987 prices. The stock has grown faster than GDP in the postwar period: it was 2.4 times GDP in 1953, when the Korean War was still in progress, and 2.8 times GDP in 1993. The private residential and nonresidential shares of the stock have been fairly stable, doubtless reflecting the long-term stability of private investment and its composition relative to the GDP. The state and local share rose until the early 1970s but has since fallen; the declining share reflects the slow growth in the public infrastructure. The federal government share is lower as a result of changes in military spending, while the consumer share has risen substantially as consumers have bought more and more automobiles and other durables. In 1993, government and consumer stocks were one-third of this aggregate.

The services yielded by private business capital are part of the GDP and are measured by the income earned in the form of profits, interest, and rents and depreciation. But that is not true of the services of durable goods held by consumers or those owned by government as GDP is now measured. Consumer stocks provide unmeasured benefits to consumers. As mentioned elsewhere, the services yielded by consumer capital stocks could be part of a GDP that was defined differently. If the definitions were changed, consumer expenditures on durable goods would be a form of investment, and on this basis, depreciation and a rate of return on this capital would have to be imputed to arrive at a flow of services from the consumer durable stock. With current definitions of GDP, similar estimates have long been made for owner-occupied housing. Extending this treatment to consumer durables would yield results superior to the present treatment in the U.S. national accounts.

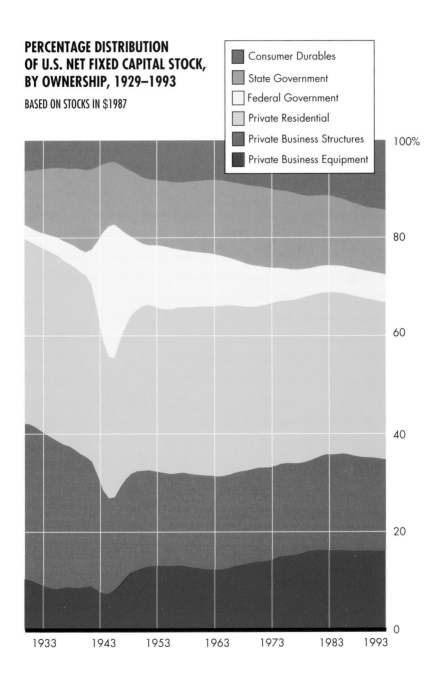

PERCENTAGE DISTRIBUTION OF U.S. NET FIXED CAPITAL STOCK, BY OWNERSHIP, 1929–1993

BASED ON STOCKS IN $1987

Legend:
- Consumer Durables
- State Government
- Federal Government
- Private Residential
- Private Business Structures
- Private Business Equipment

Government capital is often excluded in analyzing the growth of private business output. Its contribution to the growth of output and productivity remains controversial.

There is no denying that government investments yield benefits—like the increased speed and ease that individuals enjoy when traveling on our modern highway system. Benefits of this sort, however, are excluded from GDP. The practical question arises in connection with measured output: how much does government investment contribute to the long-term growth in business productivity?

Those who believe the contribution is large cite the slow growth of public infrastructure as an important factor in the slower growth of business productivity in the past twenty to twenty-five years. Critics, however, have questioned the validity of this evidence. They concede that infrastructure like the interstate highway system has reduced business costs to some extent, but they remain skeptics, citing the difficulties in measuring both benefits and costs. Government investment is not subject to the discipline of the market. For example, benefits from the public infrastructure as great as its proponents claim imply a huge rate of return on government capital. If this is so, critics ask why the public does not demand of their legislatures big new programs for public construction to be financed by higher taxes or new bond issues.

Other critics ask which way the causation runs: does reduced infrastructure investment cause slower growth of the economy, or does slower growth of the economy result in reduced spending on infrastructure?

If nothing else, potholes remind us that we need public investment and a large, rich country needs a lot of it. But with our present knowledge, economists cannot say just how important public investment is as an influence on private productivity growth.

NET CAPITAL STOCKS OWNED BY GOVERNMENTS, 1929–1993

TRILLIONS OF $1987

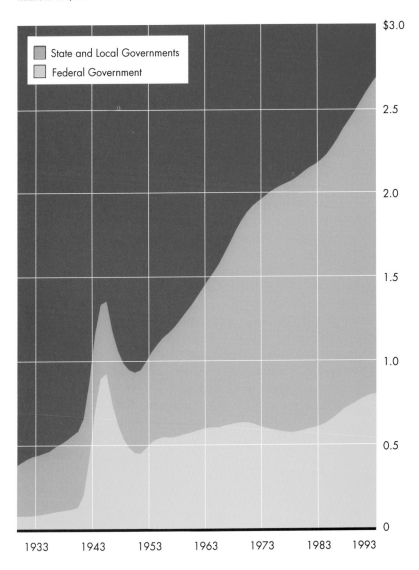

Legend:
- State and Local Governments
- Federal Government

X-axis: 1933, 1943, 1953, 1963, 1973, 1983, 1993

Y-axis: 0, 0.5, 1.0, 1.5, 2.0, 2.5, $3.0

Research and development expenditures have expanded our scientific and technological knowledge, which in turn has made a contribution to the rise in productivity.

Capital has value because it can give rise to a flow of income now and in the future, so any activity with this income-producing characteristic can be viewed as capital formation or investment.

Human capital is one form of intangible capital. Another is the "stock" of scientific and technological knowledge. Some of it is a consequence of scientific advances and great inventions like the steam engine and the computer. Economists believe that much of it is a result of research and development expenditures by private business, governments, and universities.

The chart, based on new estimates from the Commerce Department, shows business and government R&D net stocks in 1987 dollars and for comparative purposes net stocks of tangible capital of business and government. The R&D stock grew rapidly from 1959 to the early 1970s, then slowed for about a decade, but has apparently resumed a more rapid growth.

Research is important mainly because of its spillover effects, or what economists call externalities. Much basic research is of this nature because the findings of basic research are typically published in a scientific journal and are available to all rather than to a particular firm or researcher, although the patent system makes it possible for an inventor to profit from a technological breakthrough.

Although the availability of time series on R&D expenditures has encouraged economists to make estimates of the stock of research and development capital, they face many problems. Not only is the unit of research activity hard to define, but also we do not have market prices for much of the stock. How much of R&D is simply intermediate output? We do not know on any comprehensive basis how knowledge loses value with the passage of time.

A common view is that R&D is important as a source of productivity growth but just how important cannot be easily determined. R&D probably contributes more than the relatively small contribution that can be measured with a fair degree of certainty.

NET STOCK OF R&D CAPITAL COMPARED WITH TANGIBLE CAPITAL OF BUSINESS AND GOVERNMENT, 1959–1992

BILLIONS OF $1987

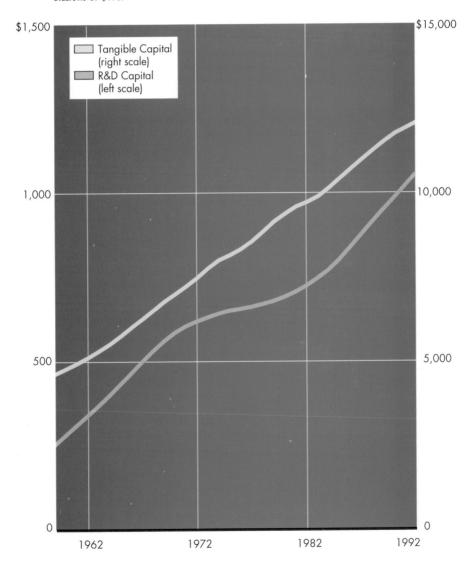

Natural resources are part
of the nation's capital.
Estimating these stocks
poses many difficulties,
but a start has
been made.

The treatment of natural resources in our national economic accounts is not very satisfactory. Important aspects of natural resources are ignored. Suppose a mineral deposit that existed at the start of a period is exhausted at the end. Whatever income was generated by the mining activity has been overstated if the exhaustion of the resource has not been accounted for. Similarly, if exploration results in a discovery, the value of the new deposit should be counted as an addition to wealth, but at present it is not.

This treatment of natural resources is very different from the way "reproducible" capital, like structures and equipment, is treated. Capital that has a long life is depreciated as it is used up, just as capital stocks are augmented when new private investment in plant and equipment is undertaken. Estimating difficulties help explain the slow statistical progress. The future yield of new discoveries is uncertain. In the 1940s and 1950s, it was common to see statements that the United States would "run out of oil" in a certain number of years. It is not easy to account for the loss of value that occurs as a resource is used up, and estimating the current value of a natural resource requires estimates of interest rates and rents, often far into the future. A comprehensive set of market prices for the natural resource might solve the valuation problems, but the price information is inadequate. In any case, such prices as exist reflect a return both on invested capital in the form of plant and equipment and on the resource in the ground. The problem is to disentangle the two.

Early in 1994, the Commerce Department took steps to set up "satellite" accounts to account for natural resources. Reflecting the many uncertainties, they made four different estimates of end of year stocks of all mineral resources (dominated by petroleum) in the United States from 1958 to 1991. The range of estimates illustrated in the chart is quite large, but the figures can at least be seen as part of the broad system of national accounts now in existence. These natural resource stocks are large: roughly $\frac{1}{2}$ trillion to 1 trillion dollars, or 3 to 7 percent of the stock of reproducible capital, at the end of 1991. In real terms, they are about unchanged from 1958 to 1991. And when these natural resources are accounted for, the return on all private capital, being spread over a bigger base, is somewhat lower than had been thought previously.

STOCKS OF SUBSOIL ASSETS BY VALUATION METHOD, 1958–1991

TRILLIONS OF $1987

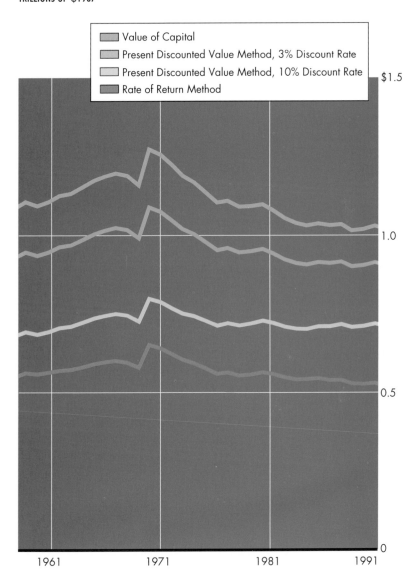

Value of Capital
Present Discounted Value Method, 3% Discount Rate
Present Discounted Value Method, 10% Discount Rate
Rate of Return Method

NOTE: See *Survey of Current Business,* April 1994, pp. 50–72.

Economists disagree about
why the nation's output
has risen faster than the
combined inputs of labor
and capital.

Although most investigators have
found that productivity change
accounts for a significant part of
the long-term rise in output, econ-
omists do not have satisfactory answers to explain what lies behind the
growth in productivity. The standard answer is "improved technology" or
"technical progress." Although this interpretation is undoubtedly correct,
economists have found this answer inadequate because it is too inclusive
and cannot itself be measured well.

The chart illustrates some 1994 findings by the Bureau of Labor Statistics for the private economy. They start off with the rise of 2.5 percent
per year in output per hour. The contribution of increased capital intensity is 0.9 percent per year. The BLS also makes an allowance of 0.2 percent
a year for the improved quality of labor (the combined influences of
education, work experience, and gender). The output rise of 2.5 percent
minus the effects of increased capital intensity (0.9) and improved labor
quality (0.2) leaves a rise of 1.3 percent (rounded) in multifactor productivity. This number is more than half the total rise in output per hour.

The BLS also presented estimates of the influence of R&D for the
nonfarm sector, which yielded a contribution of 0.2 percent per year.
Putting aside the qualifications regarding R&D mentioned earlier and
assuming that this contribution of 0.2 percent was the same in the entire
business sector including farms, we are still left with 1.1 percentage
points unexplained (1.3–0.2).

The late Edward Denison used to attach importance to the movement of resources off farms and out of small business, where they cannot
be used efficiently, into nonfarm activities. He also attached much importance to the economies of large-scale production and marketing, but
these were essentially judgmental figures rather than hard estimates.
Many other influences have been investigated, but they either have not
been very important or have lacked a solid factual basis. Taking account
of measured influences still left a large unexplained residual, variously
called "technical progress" or "advances in knowledge."

In view of these results, it seems appropriate to repeat a remark
made by Professor Moses Abramovitz many years ago. He said that the
inability of economists to measure what lies behind productivity growth
is a measure of economists' ignorance.

**CONTRIBUTION TO CHANGE IN OUTPUT
PER HOUR OF LABOR, 1948–1992**

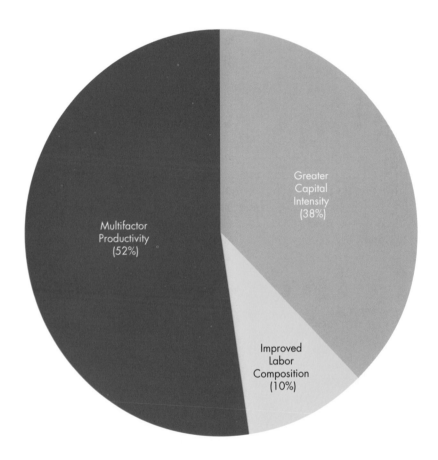

Multifactor
Productivity
(52%)

Greater
Capital
Intensity
(38%)

Improved
Labor
Composition
(10%)

Relative to GDP, the amount of domestic saving available to finance private investment has been lower in the 1980s and 1990s than earlier.

Investment has to be financed by saving, which includes not only domestic private saving but also government saving (the budget surplus) and foreign saving invested here (the capital inflow). Usually the concern for raising productivity is with private investment. If investment were defined to include government investment, the government surplus would have to be measured to exclude government investment expenditures from total government expenditures. The chart shows the domestic saving available to finance private investment. The chart on page 71 shows the effect of the flow of capital to or from the rest of the world on the availability of saving to finance investment in the United States.

Total domestic saving declined relative to GDP between the 1970s and the 1980s. A further decline in the period 1990–1993 was due at least in part, and perhaps entirely, to the recession that occupied much of those years. Between the 1970s and the 1980s, the private saving rate declined by about $4/10$ of 1 percent of GDP, and the government deficit increased by about $1^6/10$ percent of GDP, which adds to a decline of about 2 percent of GDP in the saving rate.

It is not entirely clear, however, whether one can say that the rise of the deficit caused 80 percent of the decline in savings. One theory holds that an increase in the deficit causes an increase in private saving—some would say an equal increase—because private people see the need to pay more taxes in the future to service the government debt and therefore increase their saving to prepare for that. But this force seems not to have been operative in the United States in the 1980s, since private saving did not rise to offset the rise of the budget deficit but also fell.

Another theory is that an increase in the deficit raises the demand for output, thereby increasing total output and income, and that people save more, both absolutely and relative to their income, because their income is higher.

The most common judgment is that the budget deficits made domestic saving lower than it would otherwise have been and, except insofar as they induced an inflow of capital from abroad, made investment in America lower than it would otherwise have been.

U.S. GROSS SAVING AS PERCENTAGE OF GDP, BY DECADE, 1950–1993

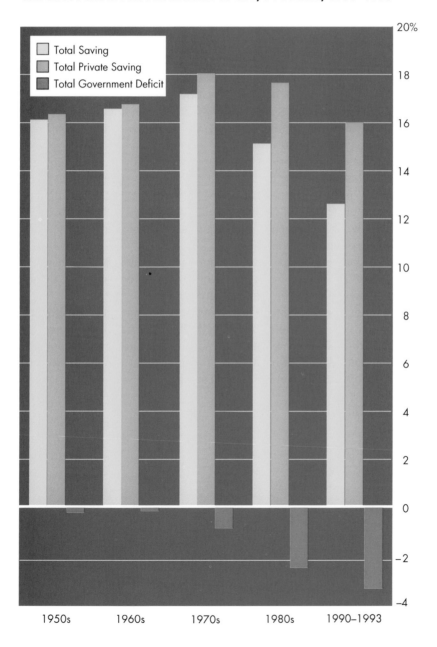

In the 1980s, and to a lesser extent in the early 1990s, private investment in America was sustained by foreign capital, despite the decline of domestic saving.

During the postwar period until the 1970s, there was a net outflow of capital from the United States to the rest of the world. A part, generally small, of U.S. saving was invested abroad. In the 1980s, that flow was reversed. Foreign capital flowed into the United States at a high rate. Instead of using part of our saving to finance investment abroad, we used part of foreign saving to finance investment here.

Between the 1970s and the 1980s, when the government deficit rose sharply, domestic saving fell from a little over 17 percent of GDP to a little over 15 percent. At the same time, the net capital inflow from abroad rose by about 2 percent of GDP (from an outflow of 0.2 percent of GDP to an inflow of 1.9 percent). This permitted domestic private investment to remain around 17 percent of GDP.

The increase of U.S. government deficits in the 1980s may have contributed to the inflow of capital that offset the adverse effect of the supply of domestic saving on domestic investment.

Although capital inflow helps support investment and the growth of productivity, in the United States a part of the resulting increase of income produced in the United States belongs to the foreign suppliers of that capital. As is shown later, the foreign-owned capital stock is still small relative to the total U.S. capital stock.

U.S. SAVING AND INVESTMENT AS PERCENTAGES OF GDP, 1950–1993

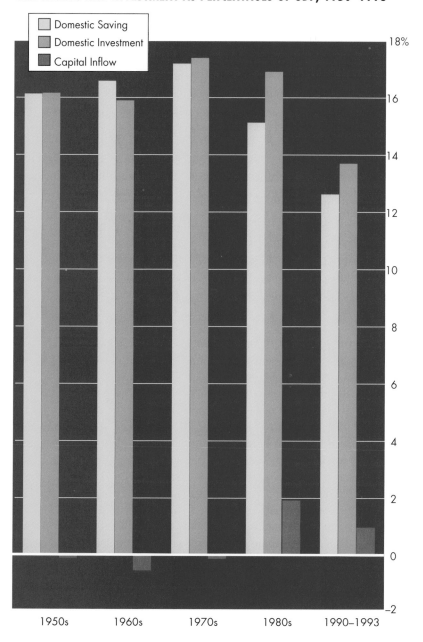

Provision for depreciation accounts for much of our gross private saving.

Gross private saving is made up of saving by households—personal saving—and saving by businesses. In 1993, personal saving was less than 20 percent of the gross private total, but in the 1960s and 1970s it was about 30 percent. Saving by business consists of two parts: retained earnings of corporations—or what corporations plow back after paying income taxes and dividends—and funds companies set aside for depreciation. Depreciation is by far the biggest component of gross private saving. Unincorporated depreciation includes not only the depreciation on buildings and equipment purchased by unincorporated businesses but also the depreciation on the stock of owner-occupied housing. In the national accounts, the homeowner is treated as a business, which rents out the premises to himself as occupant—a useful fiction for national income accounting.

Many economists prefer to measure national saving on a net rather than on a gross basis, that is, exclusive of depreciation, for the same reason that they prefer to measure production by net product rather than gross product. In this view, the relative stability of the gross saving ratio is misleading because it masks the fact that depreciation has risen relative to output while the ratio of net saving to output has declined since the 1960s. It is this aspect of private savings that has raised concerns similar to those raised about chronic government deficits, namely, that as a nation we do not save enough and consequently are not making enough provision for our capital stock.

One argument against the use of net rather than gross saving concerns the measurement of depreciation, which has always been a difficult statistical task. Very little is known about economic depreciation, that is, how different kinds of equipment and buildings lose value because of continued use and because of the appearance of superior machinery that makes the use of old machinery uneconomic. Instead, national income statisticians must rely on depreciation that companies claim for income tax purposes, with adjustments made to approximate the economic concept. The adjustments serve a useful purpose, but whether they are what is proper from an economic point of view cannot be determined easily.

GROSS PRIVATE SAVING, NET SAVING, AND DEPRECIATION AS PERCENTAGES OF GDP, 1950–1993

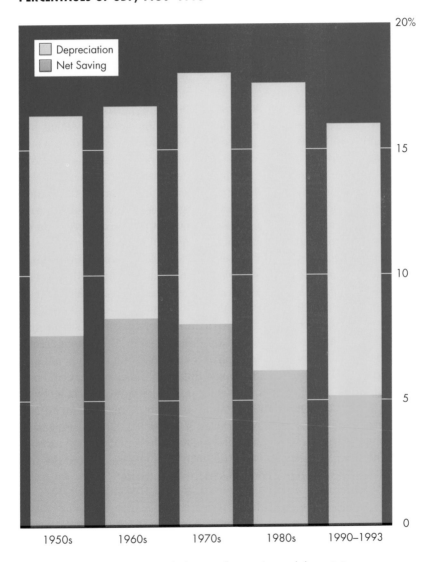

NOTE: Gross private saving equals the sum of net saving and depreciation.

The proportion of national output saved is lower in the United States than in most other large industrial countries.

The chart compares gross saving as a percentage of GDP in the United States with similar ratios in other countries for the period 1983–1992. The U.S. position would be unchanged if the comparison were limited to private saving alone. A decade or two earlier, when saving rates were higher in many countries, the U.S. private saving rate was also relatively low.

In the private sector, low rates reflect low personal saving rates. Why the U.S. rate is so low is a complex question since individuals have many motives for saving: to provide for their old age, to build up a cushion against various contingencies, to buy housing or other durables, to provide for the education of children, to leave an estate, and so on. Several investigators have found that an increased importance of the elderly in the population reduces personal saving, presumably because they no longer have a motive to save. The high level of per capita wealth in this country is undoubtedly an influence on saving.

Many things can affect differences in private saving rates among countries. At present social security contributions are treated differently from the contributions individuals make for private pension and life insurance schemes. Thus differences in the relative importance of public versus private pension systems can give rise to differences in private saving rates. Saving rates can also be affected by differences in tax systems among countries, for example, by the relative importance of income in comparison with indirect or value-added taxes. Similarly, the distribution of health and education expenditures between households and governments can affect private saving rates among countries. Countries also spend differing relative amounts on consumer durables, a factor that can affect measures of savings. Private saving rates can be altered by standardizing for these differences but not enough either to change the general rank of the United States relative to other countries or to affect trends.

GROSS SAVING AS PERCENTAGE OF GDP BY COUNTRY, 1983 TO 1992 AVERAGE

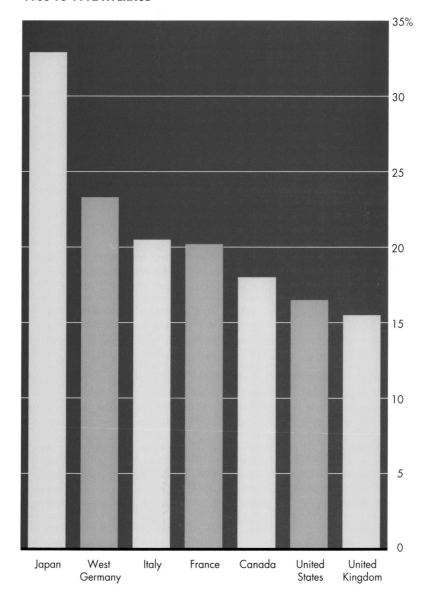

The rate of productivity growth has not been constant. The slowdown after 1973, in the United States and other countries, is not well understood.

Although output per hour of work in the private business sector grew 2.5 percent per year from 1948 to 1992, the growth has not been constant. The rate was 3.4 percent from 1948 to 1973 but only 1.3 percent from 1974 to 1992, according to the Labor Department. Productivity either declined or grew very little from 1973 to 1980. For the 1980s, the growth in productivity was higher but still well below the earlier rate. This is so whether productivity is measured by output per hour of labor (top chart) or per unit of all inputs combined (bottom chart). Over the past decade or so, slower rates of productivity growth appear in all the other leading industrial countries.

Since the mid-1970s economists have been grappling with the problem of why productivity growth has slowed down but have been unable to come up with satisfactory answers. While part of the slowdown can be accounted for, much is left unexplained; moreover, the identifiable influences are numerous rather than concentrated. Adding up what can be identified still leaves about 50 percent or more unexplained.

Although this residual has been the subject of much research and intense speculation, no consensus has formed about the causes. Some economists ask if it is valid to employ as a standard of comparison the first two decades or so after the end of World War II, since demand was unusually strong at that time. Some investigators have emphasized connections with various aspects of research and development, suggesting diminishing technological advances and lags in the use of new technology. Support for this argument has weakened.

Other possible reasons include a decline in management performance. Some investigators claim that the work ethic has deteriorated. Still others point to the misallocation of capital because of distortions caused by the tax code. A prominent explanation is the rise in energy prices in the 1970s, which made obsolete a substantial chunk of the capital stock based on cheaper energy. While some of these arguments cannot be quantified, others can be but seem unimportant in a broader framework.

Since economists have not been entirely successful in accounting for the long-term growth in productivity, it should come as no surprise that they have had only limited success in explaining the slowdown in that growth.

OUTPUT PER HOUR OF LABOR—PERCENTAGE CHANGE
FROM PRECEDING YEAR, 1949–1992

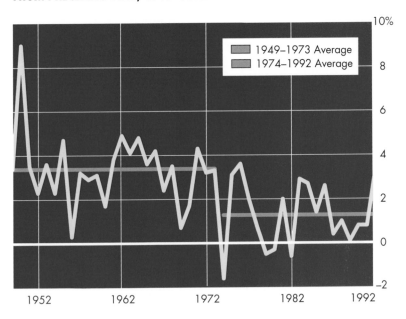

OUTPUT PER UNIT OF ALL INPUTS—PERCENTAGE CHANGE
FROM PRECEDING YEAR, 1949–1992

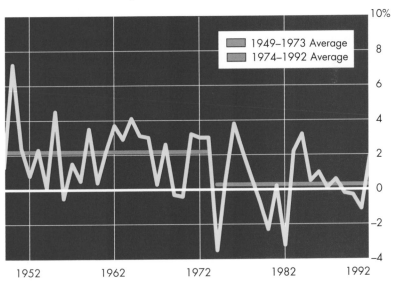

Since the early 1970s, growth in the amount of capital available to labor has also slowed down a little but not nearly so much as output per hour of labor.

One argument about the decline in productivity growth emphasizes the low rate of investment in this country. This view attributes the decline in saving over the past decade mainly to the large and continuing budget deficits of the federal government. Since the capital stock grows through additions of investment and since investment depends on saving, a reduced saving rate means a reduced rate of increase in stock of capital available for labor. (Stock of capital refers to the buildings, equipment, land, and inventories available to workers in private business.)

One problem with this argument is that the rate of growth of the capital stock did not slow down very much. The reason is that this country experienced large inflows of capital from abroad, which compensated for the low rate of national saving.

The relevant figures for analyzing this issue are output per labor hour and capital per labor hour, which are shown in the chart. The growth in capital per hour fell from an average annual rate of 3.3 percent (1948 to 1973) to 2.4 percent (1973 to 1992). Since capital has a weight of about 30 percent in this kind of accounting, it cannot explain much of the decline in labor productivity. Output per labor hour fell from a rate of 3.4 percent over the period 1948–1973 to 1.3 percent over the period 1973–1992.

Capital per worker is indeed important, as was explained earlier. But its growth is far from being the complete explanation of labor productivity growth or the slowdown in that growth.

OUTPUT AND CAPITAL PER HOUR OF LABOR IN PRIVATE BUSINESS, 1948–1992

INDEXES: 1948=100

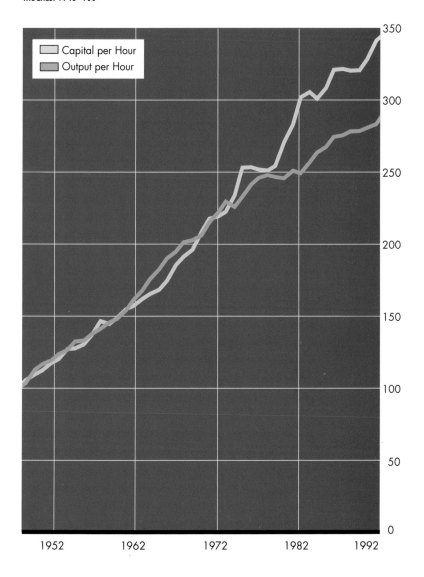

PART SIX

Labor Force and Employment

The proportion of all working-aged women who are in the work force has increased, while the corresponding proportion for working-aged men has decreased.

During the post–World War II years, strong employment growth has been accompanied by a decline in the length of the work week. The number of jobs has more than doubled since 1948. The desire of people to seek work and their ability to find work have outstripped the rise in the working-age population. About 22 percent of the labor force increase from 1948 to 1994 represents an increase in the proportion of the population in the labor force. That proportion fell from 1989 to 1992 but has begun to recover.

The civilian labor force participation rate, or the ratio of the number of persons in the labor force to the number of persons sixteen years or older, has been rising almost steadily through the postwar period. Increases among women have been large and persistent, more than offsetting decreases among men. During the 1960s the male declines were so pronounced that the combined participation rate rose slowly. In the 1970s the decrease in the male rate decelerated, while the female rate speeded up; as a result the combined rate rose very rapidly. It has since slowed down somewhat.

Several long-run factors have affected changing participation rates. For men, the greater availability and size of pension benefits have led them to retire earlier. For women, changed attitudes toward participation in the labor force and toward the age of marriage and childbearing—and the civil rights legislation of the mid-1960s—in a setting of rising labor demand have been important. Interestingly, changes in rates of participation in the labor force in this country, while not unique, are not universal. Among the large countries of the Organization for Economic Cooperation and Development, Canada has had an experience similar to ours, and that of the United Kingdom has been somewhat similar but less pronounced. Japan, Germany, France, and Italy have experienced decreases in total civilian participation rates since the 1960s, but increases have begun to appear in the past decade.

At present, civilian labor force participation rates in Canada, Japan, and the United Kingdom are either close to or a little below those in this country. Rates are considerably lower, however, in Germany, France, and especially Italy, where both men and women of working age are less likely to be in the labor force.

PARTICIPATION IN THE LABOR FORCE
BY MALES AND FEMALES, 1948–1993

PERCENT

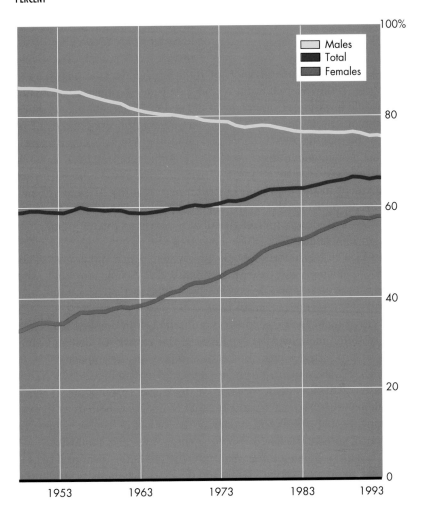

NOTE: Based on calculations of civilian labor force as percentages of population
sixteen years and over in each group.

Employment increases at different rates in different industries, and even in a period when total employment is increasing, employment in some industries is declining.

From 1980 to 1993 total private employment increased by more than 20 percent. In that period, however, employment declined in industries that in 1980 had accounted for 27 percent of total private employment. (These calculations are based on a division of total employment among sixty-five industries. If they were based on a finer division of industries the dispersion would be larger.) Employment declined by 55 percent in coal mining, for example, by 41 percent in the primary metals industry, and by 22 percent in the manufacture of electronic and other electrical equipment. In contrast, employment among security brokers increased by 110 percent, in business services by 88 percent, and in radio and TV by 83 percent. Employment in the provision of health care rose by 67 percent and in retail trade by 51 percent. The increase of employment in these two industries was almost half of the total increase in private employment between 1980 and 1993.

Still, a large proportion of all employment was in industries that had about the average increase. Industries with employment that would increase between 10 and 40 percent from 1980 to 1993 accounted for 48 percent of total employment in 1980.

Three main factors explain the differences in employment experience of different industries—changes in the pattern of demand, differences in productivity growth, and differences in the impact of foreign trade. The far-above-average increases in employment in service industries contrasted with the small increase or decline in manufacturing reflects both demand shifts and a relatively rapid growth of productivity in manufacturing. Probably the clearest sign of the impact of foreign competition was the 22 percent decline of employment in the apparel industry.

The most striking thing about this picture is the clear ability of the economy to adapt to great changes in demand, productivity, and foreign competition—affecting different industries differently—and still to maintain high employment growth and relatively little unemployment.

DISTRIBUTION OF WORKERS BY PERCENTAGE CHANGE
IN EMPLOYMENT IN THEIR INDUSTRIES, 1980–1993

% OF WORKERS

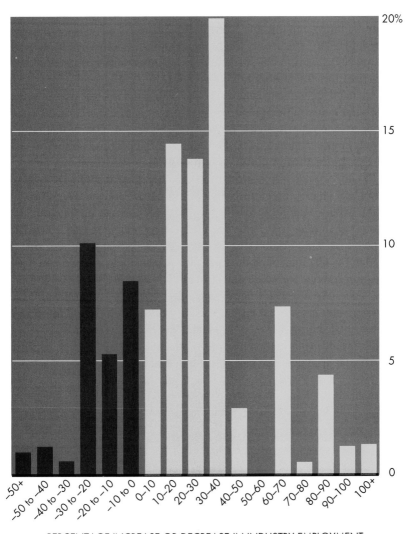

PERCENTAGE INCREASE OR DECREASE IN INDUSTRY EMPLOYMENT

As the industrial composition of jobs has changed, blue-collar jobs have declined in importance, while white-collar jobs have increased.

Not only has employment in the United States risen substantially over the postwar period, but its character has also changed. In 1948, industrial employment (manufacturing, mining, and construction) accounted for 48 percent of all wage and salary workers in the private, nonfarm sector. In 1993 that proportion had fallen to 25 percent. All the other major countries of the Organization for Economic Cooperation and Development also experienced decreasing shares in the industrial sector except Japan, where the industrial employment share increased in the early 1970s and has since fallen a little. In the European countries the absolute number of persons employed in industry declined over the postwar period.

As the relative importance of industrial employment has fallen, so has the importance of blue-collar jobs. In 1958 they accounted for 37 percent of U.S. employment; thirty-five years later, 25 percent. Over the same period white-collar jobs rose from 43 to 58 percent of the total. The importance of blue-collar jobs declined among both men and women, but the decline among women was especially large. Although women are now found in occupations once the exclusive province of men, women have a strong preference for white-collar work.

The chart does not show two other categories of workers: farm workers, who are almost all blue-collar workers and whose importance has declined sharply over the years; and "service workers," a mixed group (including household employees) whose general importance has increased a little over the past thirty-five years.

EMPLOYMENT IN BLUE- AND WHITE-COLLAR OCCUPATIONS AS PERCENTAGES OF TOTAL EMPLOYMENT, 1958–1993

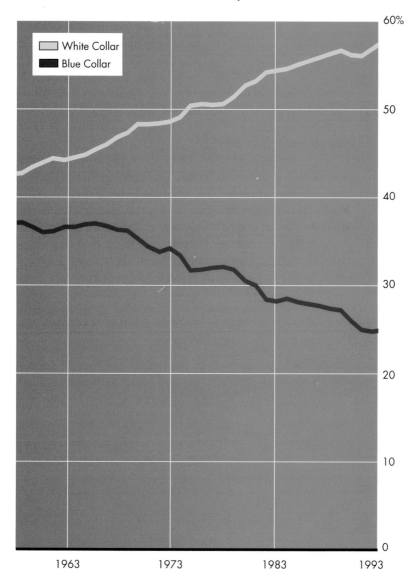

Over the past thirty years agricultural employment as a share of total employment fell sharply in the United States and much more in other industrialized countries.

Employment in agriculture in the United States was 8 percent of civilian employment in 1960 and only 2.7 percent in 1993. Declining farm employment in this country was part of a worldwide phenomenon. Over the same period, for example, all the major countries of the Organization for Economic Cooperation and Development experienced employment decreases in agriculture, and in none of the countries today is agricultural employment as much as 10 percent of the total.

What is really surprising is how large these ratios were in other countries just a generation ago: more than 30 percent in Italy, 30 percent in Japan, and 23 percent in France. One would have to go back to 1910 to find a ratio that high in the United States. As in this country, the decline in the agricultural share of employment was an important factor in the productivity rise in Western Europe, Canada, and Japan over this period. In most of those countries, however, agricultural employment is now so low that this source of productivity increase is largely spent.

AGRICULTURAL EMPLOYMENT AS PERCENTAGE OF CIVILIAN EMPLOYMENT FOR SELECTED COUNTRIES, 1960 AND 1993

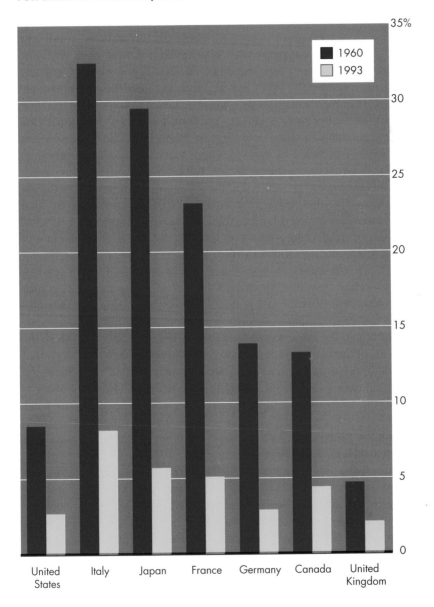

The work year has become shorter. About 7 percent of hours for which an employee is paid represents paid vacations or other paid leave.

The long-term, continuous decline in the length of the average work week and work year since the second half of the nineteenth century has lasted through the post–World War II era. The postwar decrease has reflected a shorter work week for full-time workers as well as a large increase in the proportion of workers employed part time. The lower line in the chart traces the course of average annual hours, obtained by dividing total hours by the sum of full-time and part-time employees in private nonfarm industries. The upper line divides the same aggregate hours by the number of full-time equivalent employees. (Two workers, each of whom worked half a full-time week, are considered the equivalent of one full-time worker. Full-time work schedules may vary by industry.) The difference between the two lines shows how the increased proportion of part-time workers in total employment has affected hours. Annual rates of decrease from 1948 to 1993—about 0.2 percent— are less than the annual average decline of about 0.5 percent from 1909 to 1947.

The rise in part-time employment has been large. In 1968 persons usually working part-time (less than thirty-five hours per week) constituted 14 percent of employed persons. Twenty-five years later that proportion had risen to 18 percent.

Although the labor work week in manufacturing declined from the early part of the twentieth century to the early postwar period, since that time the trend of weekly hours has been remarkably flat. The shift in the mix of industries away from manufacturing and mining toward services has had the effect of reducing the all-industry average length of the work week.

All the figures just discussed are based on the number of hours in a year for which an employee is on the job. The Bureau of Labor Statistics estimates that production workers and nonsupervisory employees in nonfarm business actually worked 93 percent of the number of hours for which they were paid in 1993. The difference represents paid vacations, holidays, and personal and administrative leave such as jury duty. For a full-time year-round job in nonfarm industries, 7 percent represents three and a half weeks of paid leave or a two-week paid vacation plus several additional days on the basis of a full-time 1993 work year of almost 1,900 hours.

AVERAGE ANNUAL HOURS PER EMPLOYEE
IN PRIVATE NONFARM INDUSTRIES, 1948–1993

HOURS

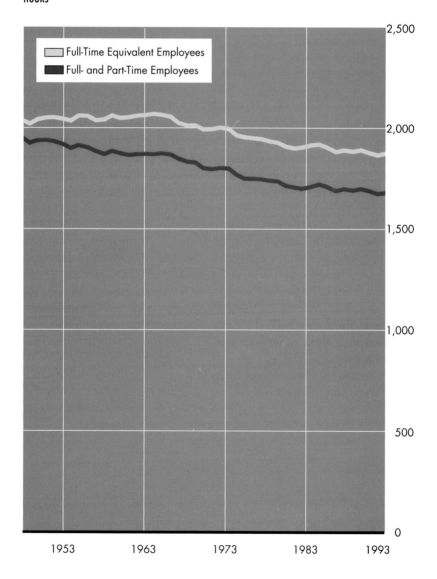

Full-Time Equivalent Employees
Full- and Part-Time Employees

2,500

2,000

1,500

1,000

500

0

1953   1963   1973   1983   1993

Increased longevity and a shorter working life have lengthened the period of retirement for men.

A baby born in 1900 had a life expectancy of only 47 years. A baby born in 1994 has a life expectancy of 75.9 years. These figures for the United States, while high, are by no means the highest in the world. Seventeen other countries had figures as high or higher, with Japan in the lead for large countries at 79.3.

At the beginning of this century a man of twenty could expect to live an additional forty-two years, during which he could expect to work thirty-eight years. The period of retirement was thus very brief. As of 1978–1980, life expectancy for an average twenty-year-old man had risen by ten years, while his expected working life was lower by one year. With a longer life expectancy and a shorter working life, the expected span of retirement rose to fifteen years, up from four years at the turn of the century. Put another way, in 1900 a man of twenty could expect to work 90 percent of his remaining life; eighty years later that proportion had fallen to 71 percent.

Life expectancy for women has risen even more than for men over this period—from forty-four to fifty-nine years for a woman of twenty. Working-life figures for women, however, have also risen, as participation of women in the labor force has gone up. In 1900 a woman of twenty could expect to be actively working in paid employment for only 14 percent of her life, but by 1979–1980 that proportion was approximately 46 percent. The average for the early period reflects a small proportion of women with work experience and a large proportion with none at all or very little.

Estimates of working-life expectancies for 1990 are not available. If they were, they would probably show a small decline for males and some increase for females. Coupled with rising life expectancies, these trends imply more leisure for men but probably not for women.

LIFE AND WORKING-LIFE EXPECTANCIES FOR MALES, TWENTY YEARS OLD, 1900–1990

NUMBER OF ADDITIONAL YEARS

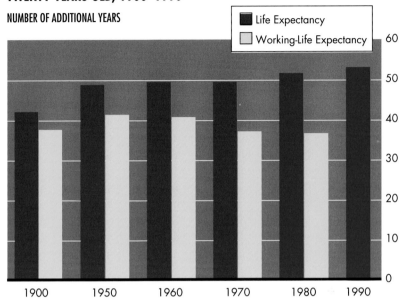

| | Life Expectancy |
| | Working-Life Expectancy |

1900   1950   1960   1970   1980   1990

LIFE AND WORKING-LIFE EXPECTANCIES FOR FEMALES, TWENTY YEARS OLD, 1900–1990

NUMBER OF ADDITIONAL YEARS

| | Life Expectancy |
| | Working-Life Expectancy |

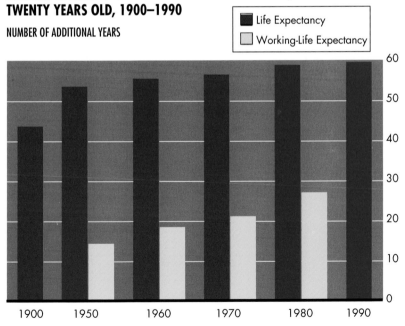

1900   1950   1960   1970   1980   1990

NOTE: Working-life expectancies not available for 1990 or for females in 1900.

Labor-force participation rates of black male teenagers have fallen, as rates for black female teenagers have risen.

Although black adult men have made genuine progress over the postwar period in entering the labor force and finding jobs, that is not true of black male teenagers. Their position with respect to the labor market has deteriorated and constitutes a serious problem for the society.

In 1960–1963, labor-force participation by black and other males in the sixteen–nineteen year age group was about the same as it was for white males of the same age. Thirty years later, this teenage white male rate was somewhat higher, while the corresponding rate for blacks had fallen and was only ²/₃ the white rate. The behavior of black males stands in contrast to the behavior of black female teenagers, whose participation rates increased over the period, although not as much as for white female teenagers.

The participation rates of both black and white male adults (aged twenty and older) fell over the period. In 1960–1963 the black male teenage rate was 64 percent of the black male adult rate. Thirty years later that proportion had fallen to 54 percent. Increased school enrollment might account for some of the decline in labor-force participation of black male teenagers from the 1960s to 1990–1993. Over this same period, however, increased school enrollment among black female teenagers did not stand in the way of increased labor-force participation.

PERCENTAGES OF MALES AGED SIXTEEN TO NINETEEN IN THE CIVILIAN LABOR FORCE, 1960–1993

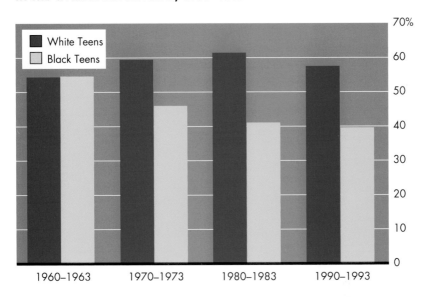

PERCENTAGES OF FEMALES AGED SIXTEEN TO NINETEEN IN THE CIVILIAN LABOR FORCE, 1960–1993

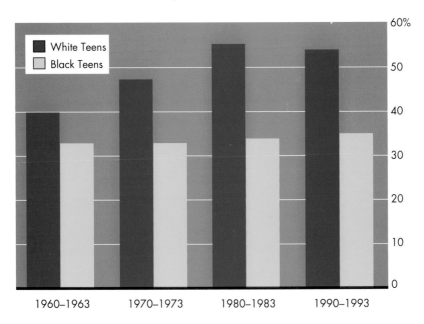

PART SEVEN

Personal Incomes

Real compensation per hour has risen roughly in line with real output per hour.

A fundamental principle of economic theory, to which most economists subscribe, is that an employer who wishes to maximize his profit will hire labor up to the point where what the worker produces is equal to the going wage. Rooted in the theory of the firm, that theory assumes that wages, prices, and technology are given and are not expected to change. In a world of changing prices and expectations, changing technology, and rigidities of all kinds, it is far from certain that the theory holds for the entire economy on an annual basis. Yet data for manufacturing as a whole and for the private business economy indicate a close relationship between trends in the movement of productivity and trends in the movement of real wages. Empirical investigations of growth in the United States make use of this principle for their theoretical underpinning.

The chart shows postwar trends in output per man-hour and real compensation per man-hour for the business sector. Real compensation per man-hour is one of several measures of real wages that might be used, as we suggest further on. The chart illustrates clearly that the slowdown in the growth of productivity since the early 1970s has its counterpart in the behavior of real compensation. The relationship holds not for short periods of time, like a year or two, but over extended periods.

The chart shows a widening gap between the growth of productivity and the growth of real wages. This gap would be less pronounced if real compensation were calculated with a different price index.

OUTPUT PER HOUR AND REAL COMPENSATION PER HOUR
IN THE BUSINESS SECTOR, 1948–1992

INDEXES: 1948=100

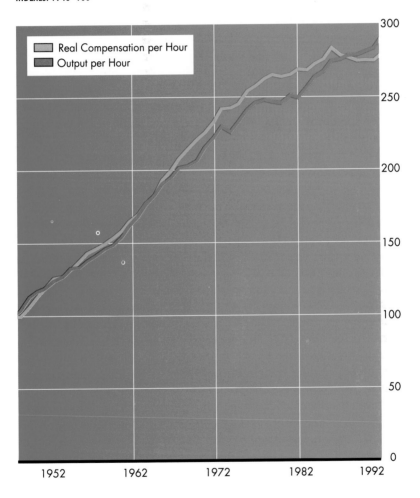

NOTE: Real compensation per hour obtained by adjusting compensation per hour with the fixed-weighted 1987 price index for personal consumption expenditures. Output per hour reflects adjustment by deflator for business output.

Different definitions and
measurements yield
different pictures of recent
developments in
real wages.

Finding out how much real wages have changed is not a simple task, because definitions vary and different measures may be found for any particular definition. A real wage is so many dollars of pay per hour or week or year divided by a price index. Several choices are available for both numerator and denominator. The numerator may refer to wages only, wages and salaries only, or wages and salaries plus fringe benefits. This last, more inclusive measure is labeled "employee compensation" in the U.S. national income accounts. Workers have shown a marked preference for additional fringes, especially health benefits, instead of straight wage increases.

When the numerator is divided by a price index applicable to a consumer market basket, we learn something about the buying power of an hour of labor of an average worker. The same numerator, though, can be divided by a price index that measures the price of what the worker has produced. The chart shows total employee compensation per hour divided by two different price indexes: the price index for personal consumption expenditures with fixed 1987 weights and the deflator for business output.

Both measures of real compensation show a considerable slowdown from 1973 to 1992 in comparison with the change from 1948 to 1973. The slowdown is more pronounced for the employee welfare measure. During the 1980s especially, the consumption price index went up more than the price of business output. The figures on compensation per hour are those used by the Bureau of Labor Statistics (BLS) in its "productivity" statistics and reflect changes in the mix of industries and occupations. From the same source we know that labor quality, measured by education and experience, has been improving. What would be the effect of holding labor quality constant? Making explicit allowance for higher labor quality from 1979 to 1992—roughly $1/2$ of 1 percent per year—suggests essentially no change in real compensation over that period if a price index for consumption is used for deflation. Calculations holding labor quality constant have their uses, but many individuals enjoy higher real incomes because of improvement in the quality of the labor they provide.

TWO MEASURES OF REAL COMPENSATION
IN THE BUSINESS SECTOR, 1948–1992

INDEXES: 1948=100

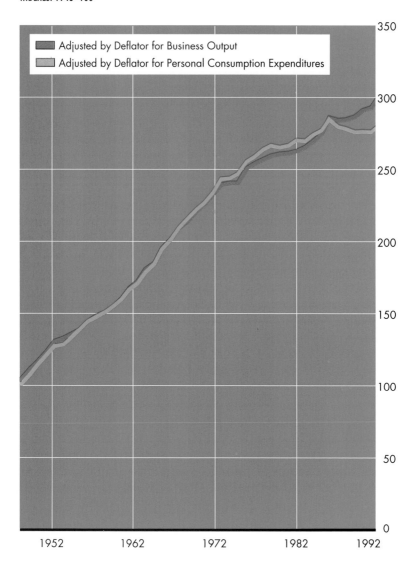

Adjusted by Deflator for Business Output
Adjusted by Deflator for Personal Consumption Expenditures

The best-known measures of real wages are the series on real average hourly earnings and the real average weekly earnings published by the Bureau of Labor Statistics (BLS). These measures, which are useful for many purposes, are not good indicators of changes in the real buying power of an hour or a week of work for the nation as a whole.

In the top chart, one line depicts the course of average hourly earnings of nonsupervisory employees in all private industries. When these are deflated by the consumer price index (CPI), they decrease at a rate of 0.7 percent a year from 1973 to 1993, after having increased at a rate of $2^{1}/_{4}$ percent a year from 1948 to 1973. The second line—real average weekly earnings—declines even more after 1973.

Both measures are different from those in the two preceding charts for several reasons. Wages and salaries have gone up less than compensation including fringe benefits from December 1980 to December 1994, 4.2 percent as against 4.7 percent per year, according to the newer BLS index of employment costs before adjustment for inflation. Before 1983 the CPI overstated the increase in consumer prices because of the way in which it measured housing costs, a fault commonly ignored in long-term comparisons. Finally, weekly earnings have declined, partly because many workers choose to work a short week.

The bottom chart on the facing page illustrates four measures of real compensation per hour worked from 1959 to 1993. They demonstrate how results are affected by the choices made for the numerator (the wage) and the denominator (the price index).

The chart has two coverage variants—all employees (public as well as private) and private employees only—and two price index variants. One uses an index with fixed 1987 weights, the other an index whose weighting is updated about every five years. These are the main points:

• All four measures rise since 1973, but much more slowly than before.

• The changing-weight measures rise less than the fixed weights.

• The rise for all employees exceeds that for private employees.

CONVENTIONAL MEASURES OF REAL EARNINGS IN PRIVATE NONAGRICULTURAL INDUSTRIES, 1947–1993

INDEXES: 1982=100

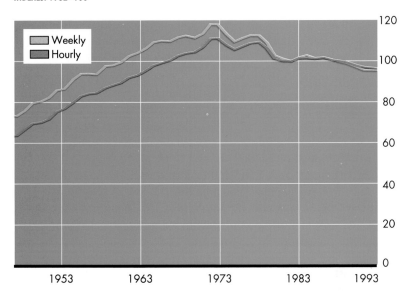

FOUR MEASURES OF REAL HOURLY COMPENSATION, 1959–1993

INDEXES: 1959=100

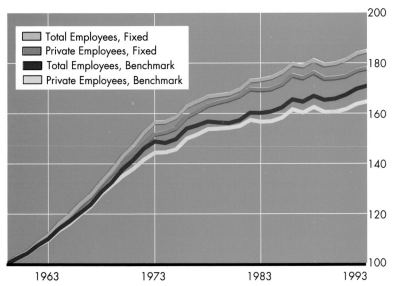

NOTE: "Fixed" and "Benchmark" refer to weights used for price indexes (see text).

Slower productivity growth is reflected in a slower rise in family income. Taking account of smaller family size and using more appropriate price measures improve the results.

Since the growth of real labor compensation per hour or year has slowed down, the growth of any other income measure consisting mainly of labor compensation—like the income of most families—also exhibits a slowdown. When Census Bureau data from the Current Population Survey on median family cash income are deflated by the consumer price index (CPI), they show a decrease from 1973 to 1992. But these results must be qualified. The price rise is overstated by use of the CPI, as was already pointed out. In addition, family size has gone down, from 2.8 persons in 1973 to 2.4 persons in 1992. Also, these calculations understate income insofar as they do not count income in kind, like food stamps, Medicare payments, employer contributions to private pension funds, and health insurance provided by employers. In contrast, these particular data overstate the level of income by using a before-tax measure of income rather than an after-tax measure.

The Congressional Budget Office (CBO) recalculated changes in family real income after making two adjustments: using a better price index and taking into account the change in family size. (In 1983 the BLS improved its method of calculating changes in housing costs. This method is reflected in an alternative BLS price index, CPI-U-X1, which goes back to 1967.) With these adjustments now updated to 1992, we find instead of a decline there is a rise in family income of about 9 percent from 1973. Income reached a peak in 1989 and declined about 5 percent from 1989 to 1992. The decrease since 1989 reflects the recession and the weak recovery in 1991 and 1992.

Preliminary data point to a further decrease in real family income in 1993, despite some acceleration in the pace of the business-cycle upturn. The 1993 figures, however, which were collected in March 1994, reflect many changes in the Current Population Survey, which may have affected the measurement of family income. Even if this is so, it is hard to escape the conclusion that real family income has not grown much in the past twenty years and has grown much less than it did in the first two or three decades after the end of World War II.

MEDIAN FAMILY INCOME, WITH ADJUSTMENTS, 1973–1992

INDEXES: 1973=100

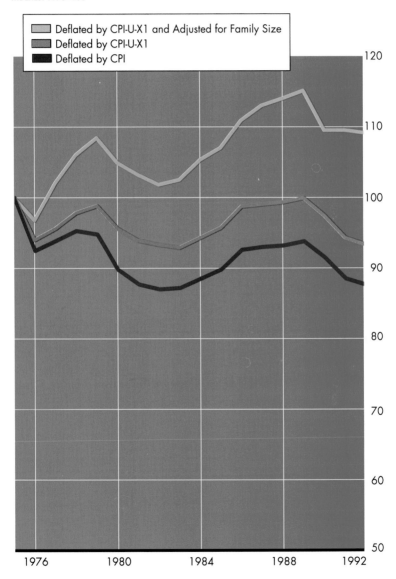

Deflated by CPI-U-X1 and Adjusted for Family Size
Deflated by CPI-U-X1
Deflated by CPI

PART EIGHT

Distribution of Income

As has been true in all times and all places, the distribution of income in the United States is unequal. The change in the United States in the past twenty years is hard to interpret.

The universally observed inequality in the distribution of income reflects the unequal distribution of the factors that yield income— personal productivity, attitudes toward work and saving, inherited wealth, power, and luck. For the distribution of income after taxes and including government benefit payments, the size and character of those elements may also be significant.

By the most commonly cited evidence, the distribution of income in the United States has become more unequal in the past twenty years or so. The chart facing shows estimates of the distribution of family cash income after tax plus in-kind food and housing benefits. Adjustment is also made for the size of families. Estimates on the same basis are not available for earlier years, but estimates of the distribution of pretax cash income show that there was an increase in inequality of annual income from 1967 to 1992 as well.

An important qualification to the figures shown here is that they relate to the income received in a single year, whereas income received over a longer period, up to a lifetime, is certainly more equally distributed and more significant for the measure of family welfare.

The inequality of annual incomes is in part a matter of age. Even if everyone had the same income over his or her lifetime, annual incomes would be unequal because people in their prime working years, say from forty-five to fifty-five years of age, would earn more than younger and older people. This is illustrated later in this chapter. Several factors have been affecting the distribution of income. The additional income earned for additional education has increased, and since the higher-income people tend to be the better educated, that has increased their relative income. Change in family structure is also important. The lowest quintile is increasingly populated by families headed by young unmarried women with low productivity, while the highest quintile is increasingly populated by families with two employed and educated adults.

Other factors have worked to decrease inequality over the recent past. Inequality in the incomes of whites and blacks, and of men and women, of comparable educational attainment has diminished.

SHARES OF TOTAL INCOME OF ALL FAMILIES
AFTER TAXES AND BENEFITS, 1979–1992

% OF TOTAL INCOMES

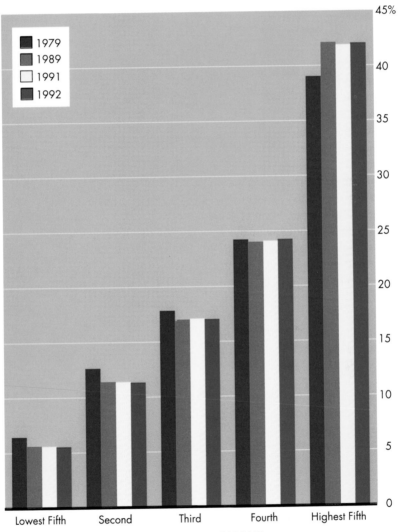

FAMILIES RANKED BY INCOME

The income of households
when counted over a
period longer than a year
is less unequally
distributed than annual
income and may not be
becoming more unequal.

A household's annual consumption may be a better reflection of its average income over several years than its income in any particular year is. If a household's income falls in one year it is likely not to reduce its consumption expenditure to the same degree, especially if the decline in income is expected to be temporary. The household will tend to adjust its consumption expenditures to its income over a longer period, borrowing or saving less when income is temporarily low, saving more when income is unexpectedly high. The chart shows estimates of the distribution of total consumption expenditures. According to these estimates, the share of consumption expenditures made by the households in the lowest fifth of all households did not change between 1971 and 1991, suggesting that the figures on annual income alone may overstate considerably the relative decline in the condition of the least well off.

Some estimates of the incomes of individual households over ten-year periods, derived from small samples, also show much less inequality than is shown in the annual income figures but still some increase of inequality.

SHARES OF TOTAL HOUSEHOLD EXPENDITURE, BY QUINTILES, 1961–1991

% OF TOTAL EXPENDITURES

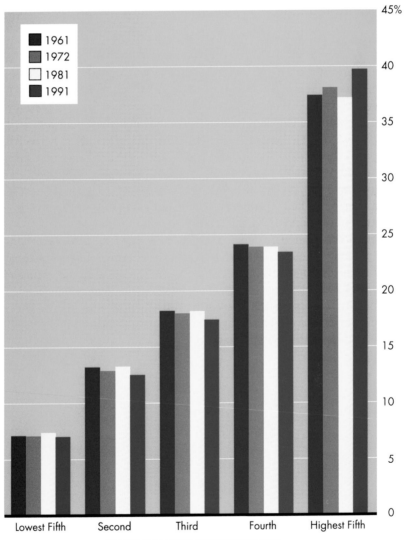

The incomes of both
younger and older
householders have
declined relative to the
incomes of householders
in their prime
earning years.

Household heads aged forty-five to fifty-four typically have higher earnings than either younger or older household heads. That is natural, since the younger ones have less experience and education than the middle-aged ones, and many of the older ones are wholly or partially retired. These disparities have increased greatly since the end of World War II. In 1947 the median income of a household headed by a fifteen- to twenty-four-year-old was almost 70 percent as high as that of a household headed by a forty-five- to fifty-four-year-old. In 1992 the ratio was only 31 percent. This is partly the result of the increased premium on experience and education that has occurred in the postwar period. But also, and probably more important, the fifteen- to twenty-four-year-old household heads are younger, and a larger proportion of them are female, than in 1947. In fact, between 1973 and 1992, the median income declined by 34 percent in households headed by persons fifteen to twenty-four years of age and by 10 percent in households with twenty-five- to thirty-four-year-old heads.

The decline in the relative incomes of the older groups is much less marked. Especially for the fifty-five- to sixty-four-year group, the decline probably reflects the trend to earlier retirement. It may also be true that the older groups on the average received less education when young than the forty-four- to fifty-four-year group did.

MEDIAN INCOME OF HOUSEHOLD, BY AGE OF HOUSEHOLDER, 1947, 1973, AND 1992

INCOME OF HOUSEHOLDS HEADED BY 45- TO 54-YEAR-OLDS=100

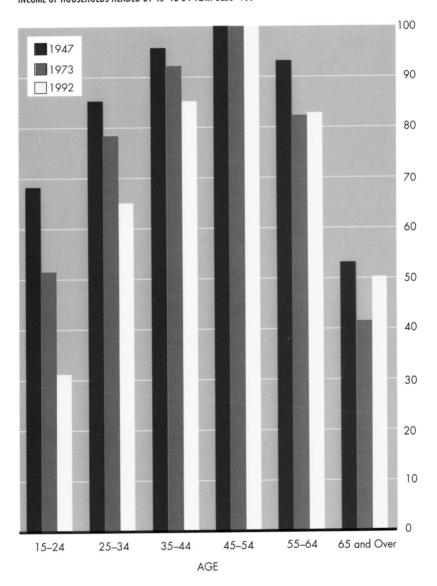

In the postwar period, the
wages of black male
workers rose substantially
relative to the wages of
whites, but a significant
gap remains.

In 1940 the average black male worker with twelve years of schooling earned about 56 percent as much as a white male with the same number of years of schooling. By 1980 that ratio had risen to 79 percent. There were similar gains for workers with other amounts of schooling.

This narrowing of the gap of earnings was due in part to a reduction in the gap in the quality of the schooling of blacks compared with whites having equal years of schooling. And probably some improvement occurred in the quality of the work experience enjoyed by blacks with the same education as whites. These factors are suggested by the second chart on the facing page. In 1940 a black with twelve years of schooling who had entered the labor force between 1900 and 1910 earned $.36 for every $1.00 earned by a white in the same condition. But if the black worker had entered the labor force sometime in the 1930s, he earned $.70 for every $1.00 the white worker earned. By 1980 this difference between date of schooling or years of experience mattered very little. Evidently the significance of differences in the quality of schooling or of work experience had greatly diminished.

Between 1980 and 1990 the gap between the earnings of blacks and whites changed very little. This is sometimes interpreted as a sign that the process of declining discrimination has come to an end. There is, however, another possible explanation. Since the 1980s the gap between the earnings of less skilled and more skilled persons—with the same years of schooling and experience—has widened, for both whites and blacks. If, as is probable, the blacks on the average were less skilled than the whites because of earlier qualitative differences in schooling and experience, then the widening of the skill differential would have caused a decline of black earnings relative to whites. The fact that this did not happen suggests that this factor was being offset by a continuing decline in discrimination.

WAGES OF BLACK MALES AS PERCENTAGE OF WAGES OF WHITE MALES, BY YEARS OF EDUCATION, 1940, 1980, AND 1990

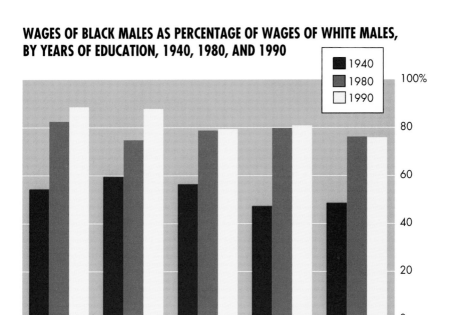

NOTE: 1990 data reflect 0–8 years and 8 to 11 years.

WAGES OF BLACK MALES AS PERCENTAGE OF WAGES OF WHITE MALES, BY YEARS IN THE LABOR FORCE, 1940, 1980, AND 1990

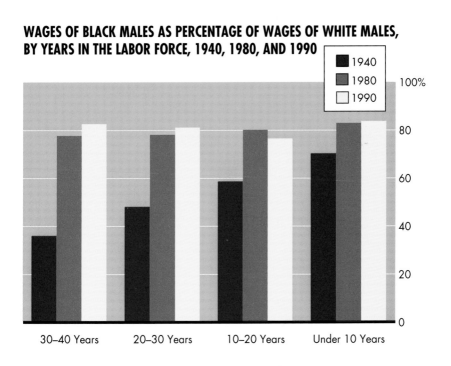

The earnings of workers with more schooling have increased substantially relative to the earnings of workers with less schooling.

In 1979 a male with sixteen years of schooling earned 45 percent more than one with twelve years of schooling. By 1993 the excess had risen to 62 percent. The relative increase was even greater for males with more than sixteen years of schooling. At the same time the earnings of males with fewer than twelve years of schooling fell relative to those with twelve years. For women the changes were in the same direction, but the relative decline among the less-educated was greater and the relative rise among the more-educated was smaller.

The figures cited here and shown in the chart refer to year-round, full-time workers aged thirty-five to forty-four years, but the picture would not be different for other age groups. The figures are also based on earnings excluding fringe benefits. Data on total compensation of persons with different educational attainments are not available. Still, there is little doubt that the total compensation of workers with little schooling lagged behind that of workers with more schooling, even if we do not know the precise quantities.

Technological change and shifts of demand toward occupations requiring more skilled workers were the main factors in this development. Increasing foreign competition in markets for goods whose production requires little education may have played a part, although attempts to measure the importance of this factor have not found it to be large.

MEAN EARNINGS OF MALES, 1979 AND 1993

AS PERCENTAGE OF MALES WITH TWELVE YEARS OF SCHOOLING

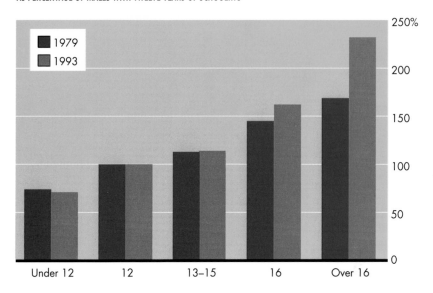

MEAN EARNINGS OF FEMALES, 1979 AND 1993

AS PERCENTAGE OF FEMALES WITH TWELVE YEARS OF SCHOOLING

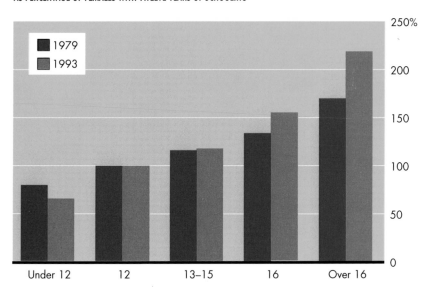

The 1980s saw a resumption of the long-term trend for the wages of working women to come closer to those of working men.

Between 1890 and 1955 the ratio of women's wages to men's rose from about 45 percent to about 65 percent. This resulted from the rise of the educational attainment of women and from the decline of the discrimination against the entry of women into some of the higher-paid occupations. Also, technological change reduced the relative earnings in jobs requiring much physical strength, which were mainly men's jobs.

In the 1960s and 1970s the ratio of women's wages declined a little. The number of women in the labor force was rising much more rapidly than the number of men, so that the number of workers with little work experience rose more rapidly among women than among men. This decline in relative work experience offset, for a time, the effect of the longer-term factors that were raising the relative earnings of women. That reduced the average earnings of women relative to the average earnings of men. Since 1980 the factors of increasing relative education, declining discrimination, and changing technology, which all tend to raise the relative earnings of women, have again dominated, and the ratio of women's to men's earnings has reached a new high.

The earnings of older women are usually lower, relative to the earnings of men of the same age, than is true for younger women. In part this reflects the fact that the difference in continuous work experience, which adds to skills and earnings, is greater between older men and women than between younger men and women. But it is probably also true that the women who entered the labor force thirty years ago had less education and embarked on less promising career tracks than the women who entered the labor force more recently.

RATIO OF WOMEN'S TO MEN'S EARNINGS, MEDIAN EARNINGS OF FULL-TIME, YEAR-ROUND WORKERS, 1890–1990

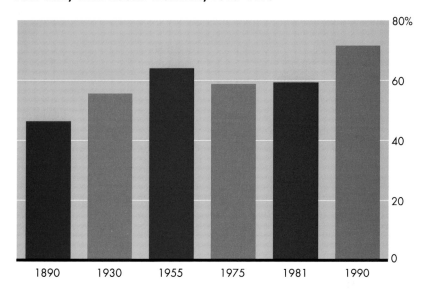

NOTE: Intervals between bars are unequal.

HOURLY EARNINGS OF WOMEN AS PERCENTAGE OF HOURLY EARNINGS OF MEN, BY YEARS OF AGE, 1979 AND 1992

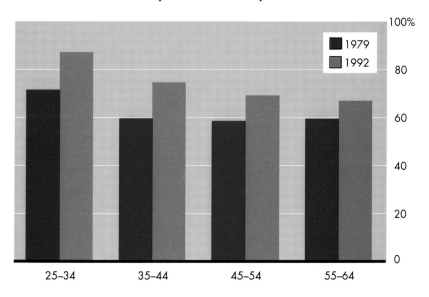

Differences in income per person among states are large.

In 1993 per capita income in Connecticut, the top state, was $28,000 or 134 percent of the U.S. average, while income in Mississippi, the bottom state, was $14,700, or 71 percent of the national average. Focusing on the top five and the bottom five states would narrow the spread somewhat, but not much. Nor are extremes the whole story. The middle part of the distribution is large: for example, more than half the states have per capita incomes that fall within 15 percent of the national average.

The economic well-being of the average resident of the various states depends on things besides before-tax income, namely, the burden of taxes and what it costs to live in different places. The only tax figures available on a basis consistent with the income data are income taxes (federal, state, and local). The pattern of after-tax incomes does show some differences from the before-tax pattern, since state income tax rates vary among the states. By and large, though, the picture is not very different. Federal income taxes, which are common to all the states, accounted for three-quarters of combined federal, state, and local income taxes in 1993. A more accurate analysis would also take account of sales and property taxes.

Current figures on what it costs to live in different states are not available. The Bureau of Labor Statistics used to publish comparisons of what it would cost to maintain a "moderate urban living standard" for a four-person family and a two-person retired couple in each of several dozen metropolitan areas. The figures are no longer available and in any case were limited in scope. About all one can say is that differences in per capita incomes among states would be reduced but would still remain after taking living costs into account.

PERSONAL INCOME PER PERSON
FOR THE HIGHEST AND LOWEST STATES, 1993

THOUSANDS OF $

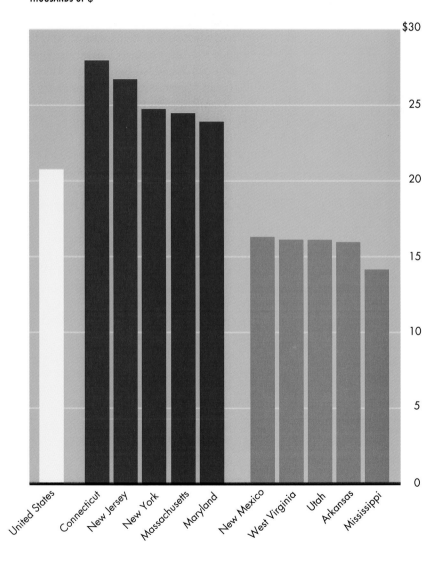

Regional disparities
in income per person
have tended to
decrease. From 1929 to 1979 differences in
state per capita incomes grew
smaller. Trends that were evident in the 1930s were greatly accelerated in
the decade of the 1940s and continued at a slower but steady pace for the
next three decades. In the 1980s, however, these trends seem to have been
reversed. It may be that the experience of the 1980s was an aberration,
because in 1993 the regions seemed to be reverting to the pre-1980 pattern.

The chart, taken from one published earlier by the Bureau of
Economic Analysis, illustrates these movements in very summary form.
States are divided into eight regions. Regions are defined once as "high"-
income or "low"-income, depending on whether they are above or below
the U.S. average for all states. In 1929 the high group was 127 percent of
the U.S. average, and the low group 64 percent. By 1950 those differences
had become 114 and 81, and by 1979, 107 and 90. But in 1989 the figures
were 109 and 88, and in 1993, 108 and 91.

These numbers show how much the low-income regions—the
South in particular—have improved relative to the rest of the country.
While incomes are still below average in the South, that region can no
longer be viewed as it was as recently as twenty-five years ago.
Economists, however, look not only at the improvement of the low-
income regions but also at the relative decline of the high-income areas.
According to conventional economic theory, these results are to be
expected where resources are free to move, as they are in the United
States.

Businesses, for example, are attracted to low-cost areas, where they
invest in new, productive facilities, and these investments in turn permit
higher wages. Many older areas in the Northeast and Midwest, where basic
industries were dominant, have either declined or stagnated. The theory
probably explains a good part of the broad pattern over the long run, but
the experience of the 1980s may call for a more complex explanation.

INCOME PER PERSON AS PERCENTAGE OF THE U.S. AVERAGE FOR HIGH AND LOW PERSONAL INCOME REGIONS, 1929–1993

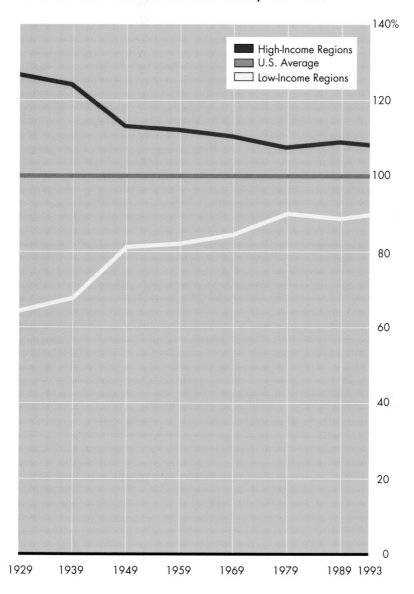

PART NINE
Poverty

There is no objective definition of *poverty* and no objective way of measuring how many people are in poverty. The numbers differ greatly according to different plausible definitions.

The term *poverty* generally implies not only having less income than someone else or less income than the recipient would like. It means an economic condition of sufficient concern to call for extraordinary action to correct it—either by the government or by someone else. Judgments about what that condition is differ widely. Since 1963 there has been an "official" definition of poverty in the United States, namely, having an income less than three times the cost of a minimally adequate diet for a family of a given size, the required income being adjusted each year for change in the price level. In 1993 the poverty line for a family of four was $14,763.

Many other reasonable definitions of poverty would give estimates of the proportion of the population in poverty very different from the official one. (These figures relate to 1987, later ones on the same definitions not being available, but the basic point of the differences in estimates resulting from definitions remains valid.) The standards in the chart opposite are:

A.   the official standard—cash income below the official threshold of three times the cost of minimal food needs in 1963 adjusted by change in the consumer price index

B.   same as A but including as income food, housing, and medical benefits valued at market cost

C.   same as B but valuing in-kind benefits, such as medical care, at estimated worth to the recipient

D.   same as B but excludes medical benefits from income

E.   same as C but excludes medical benefits from income

F.   same as A but 1963 threshold adjusted by a corrected consumer price index

G.   same as A but original threshold adjusted by increase in median income rather than by price index

H.   cash income below 50 percent of median income

I.   cash income below estimated requirements for minimal housing needs

J.   cash income below estimated current requirements relative to minimal food needs, which is a larger multiple of food costs than in 1963

U.S. POVERTY RATE ACCORDING TO TEN STANDARDS OF POVERTY, 1987

% OF U.S. POPULATION BELOW POVERTY LINE

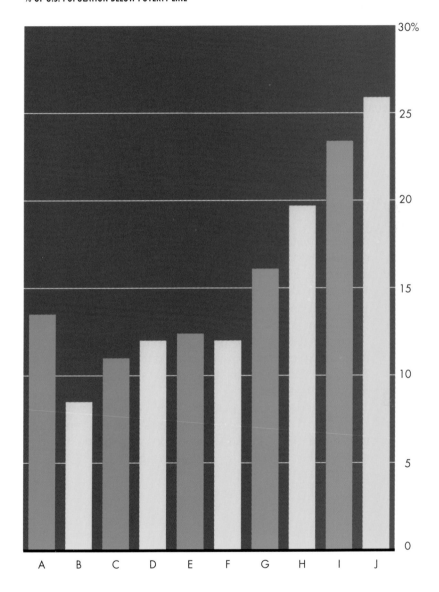

Estimates of the poverty population by the Census Bureau on several definitions show similar trends since 1979.

The Census Bureau calculates the number of people in poverty under a number of definitions, although not all of those that are shown in the preceding chart. We show here the estimates of the poverty rate by years from 1979 according to three definitions. The middle line refers to the official definition. The top line, labeled *Variant A*, shows the rate under the definition that would show the most poverty, which is pretax cash income excluding all government transfers. The bottom line, labeled *Variant B*, shows the rate under the definition that would show the least poverty, which includes as income not only all cash transfers, such as social security benefits, but also noncash transfers, such as Medicare and Medicaid, and the imputed rental value of an owner-occupied home.

The trend of poverty over the period 1979 to 1993 is much the same in the three variants, and that is true also of other variants calculated by the Census Bureau.

Other possible definitions would yield estimates of the size of the poverty population even smaller than the lowest shown in the chart. The estimates shown here refer to the status of a household each year, whereas a household that falls below the poverty line in only one of several years may not be really poor. For the ten years from 1969 to 1978, only 2.6 percent of the population was poor in eight years out of ten. The number of people counted as being in poverty would also be smaller than shown in the common measurements if consumption rather than income were used as the standard, since poor families typically spend more than their reported income on consumption.

Despite these uncertainties about the definition and measurement of poverty at any time, the official measurements probably provide an adequate indication of the relative distribution of poverty and of its trend over time, which will be shown in the following pages.

CENSUS MEASUREMENTS OF POVERTY
AS PERCENTAGE OF U.S. POPULATION, 1979–1993

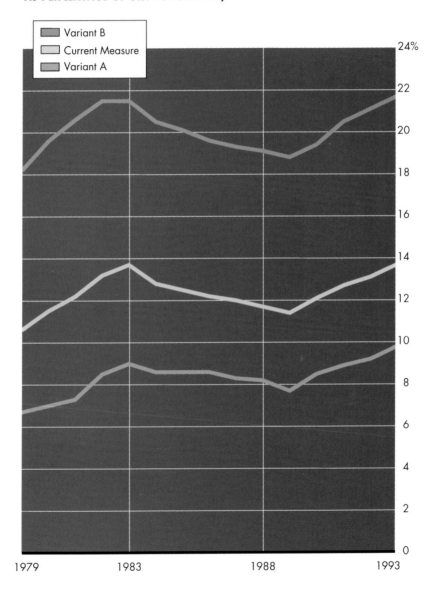

The proportion of the population living in poverty fell sharply during the 1960s but has fluctuated with the business cycle and may even have risen slightly since.

The figures charted here are for the "official" definition of poverty, which draws the line at three times the cost of an estimated minimal diet. Although there are no calculations on the same basis for years before 1959, it seems clear that the decline of poverty had been going on for a long time. One study has estimated that the proportion of families in poverty fell by 50 percent between 1929 and 1960. Another estimated that the proportion of families in poverty fell from 67 percent in 1896 to 17 percent in 1965. This is the result to be expected in an economy where average real incomes are rising and where the dividing line between poverty and not-poverty is an absolute level of real income. If the distribution of income remains roughly constant, the rise in average incomes implies a rise in the incomes of the poorest also.

The failure of the poverty rate to decline after about 1973 is difficult to explain. Real per capita incomes were not rising as fast as they had done earlier in the postwar period, but they did rise as fast between 1973 and 1993 as between 1929 and 1958, when the poverty rate did decline substantially. The failure of poverty to decline in recent years does not seem to be a peculiarity of the particular definition used here. The Bureau of the Census calculated poverty rates according to fifteen definitions from 1979 to 1992, and although these calculations show markedly different levels in 1992, they all show some increase between 1979 and 1992. Part of the explanation for the behavior of the poverty rate lies in changes in family structure, especially the rise in the number of female-headed families.

Starting from a much higher level in 1959, the poverty rate among blacks followed much the same path as that of whites. It fell sharply until about 1973 and has fluctuated mildly around a slightly rising trend since. The black poverty rate has remained about three times the white rate.

PERCENTAGE OF POPULATION IN POVERTY, BY RACE, 1959–1993

OFFICIAL DEFINITION

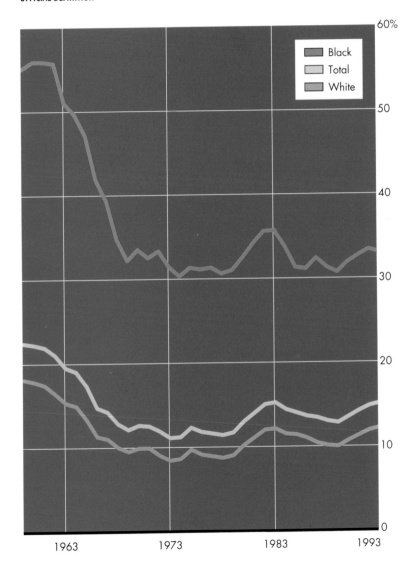

Poverty in America has increasingly become a problem of persons in households headed by females.

In 1968, 28 percent of the people in America with incomes below the poverty line were in families headed by women. By 1993 this proportion had risen to 37 percent, although not because the proportion of female-headed families who were poor had increased. In fact, that proportion, although higher than for the rest of the population, was just as high in 1968 as in 1993. The proportion of the population in female-headed families had increased, however, from 9 percent to 15 percent.

The other big change in the distribution of poverty in America was the sharp drop in the proportion of the poverty population who were above sixty-five years of age—from 18 percent to 10 percent. This change occurred despite some increase in the proportion of the elderly in the total population. The drop resulted from a decline in the proportion of the elderly who were poor, from 25 percent in 1968 to 12 percent in 1993. Social security undoubtedly contributed to this decline, but so did private savings and pensions.

The largest part of the population is neither elderly nor in female-headed households. The poverty rate of the rest of the population increased from 8.5 percent to 11 percent between 1968 and 1993, and they continued to constitute a majority of the poverty population.

If the poverty rates in each of the three population groups shown here had remained constant at their 1968 levels, and the composition of the total population had changed as it did, then the total poverty rate would have increased from 12.8 percent in 1968 to 14.8 percent in 1993. It actually increased to 15.1 percent.

COMPOSITION OF POVERTY POPULATION
AS PERCENTAGE OF TOTAL, 1968 AND 1993

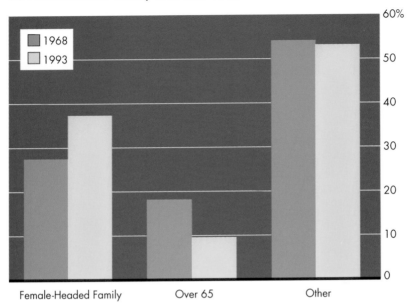

- 1968
- 1993

Female-Headed Family | Over 65 | Other

PROPORTIONS OF GROUPS IN POVERTY, 1968 AND 1993
PROPORTION OF CLASS IN POVERTY

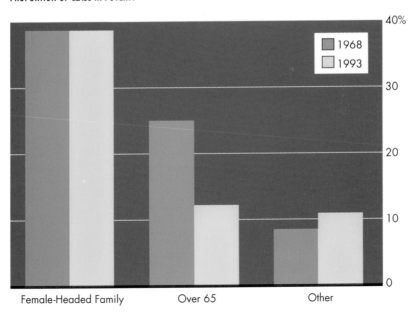

- 1968
- 1993

Female-Headed Family | Over 65 | Other

The proportion of children in poverty, by the official definition, is much higher than for adults and has been increasing.

In 1993, when 15 percent of the population was estimated to have been in poverty, almost 23 percent of children (persons under eighteen) were estimated to have been in poverty. Child poverty has increased substantially as a fraction of the number of children and also as a fraction of the total poverty population, largely because of the increased concentration of poverty in families headed by single women.

The proportion of children in poverty is much higher for blacks than for whites, but the ratio of child poverty to total poverty is about the same for blacks as for whites.

PERCENTAGE OF WHITE CHILDREN AND BLACK CHILDREN IN POVERTY, 1974–1993

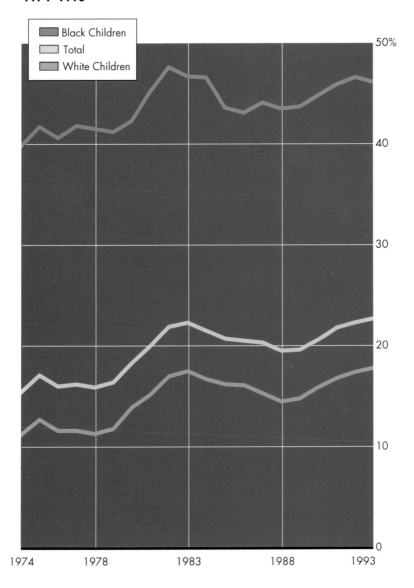

The poverty population includes a smaller group, sometimes called the "underclass," that constitutes a special problem.

To say that a person is "in poverty" commonly suggests that he not only has a low income but also lives in a community characterized by extremely bad economic functioning. That is true, however, of only a small fraction of the Americans officially counted as being in poverty. That fraction is sometimes called an "underclass," referring to permanent features not of the persons themselves but of the environment in which they are living.

One definition of underclass is, people living in neighborhoods where there are significantly above-average proportions of (a) men not attached to the labor force, (b) teenagers who are high school dropouts, (c) families headed by women with children, and (d) households dependent on welfare. The top chart facing shows the proportions of the total U.S. population and of whites and blacks separately who were in the underclass by this definition in 1970, 1980, and 1990. These numbers are much smaller than the proportion of the population in poverty. In 1990 only 3¾ percent of all poor people lived in underclass areas, about 1¼ percent of the white poor and 8¾ percent of the black poor. Although the proportion of the black population counted as being in poverty was about three times as high as the proportion of whites, the proportion of blacks living in underclass areas was fourteen times as high as the proportion of whites.

The bottom chart facing gives a different picture of the extent to which Americans live in communities of extraordinary economic distress. It shows the proportion of the total population, and of whites and blacks separately, living in areas where more than 40 percent of the population is poor. For the total population these figures are about four times as high as the numbers in the underclass, and for blacks also they are about four times as high.

By both measures the proportion of the population living in distressed areas increased between 1970 and 1990. The proportion counted in the underclass, however, declined between 1980 and 1990. That was mainly because a decline in school dropout rates removed a number of areas from the "underclass" category.

PERCENTAGE OF POPULATION LIVING IN "UNDERCLASS" AREAS, 1970, 1980, AND 1990

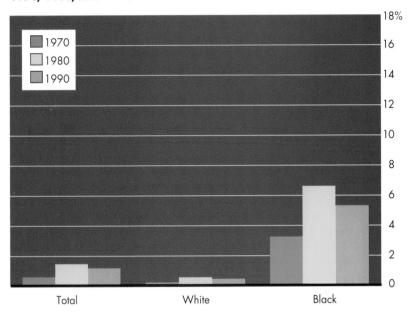

PERCENTAGE OF POPULATION LIVING IN AREAS OF CONCENTRATED POVERTY, 1970, 1980, AND 1990

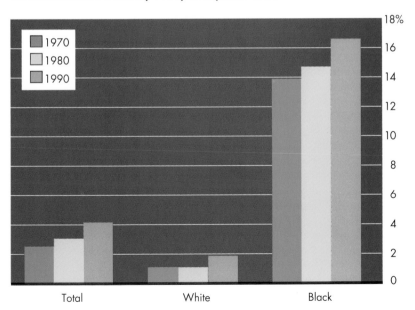

PART TEN
The Structure of
the Economy

More than half of U.S. workers are employed in firms with fewer than 500 employees. In manufacturing, the importance of the largest firms varies, depending on the criterion used to measure size.

Small business occupies a prominent place in the public policy agenda of this country, a position that was formalized by the creation of the Small Business Administration in 1953. Small business is not an economic term: what is small in one industry may be very large in another. For practical reasons the Small Business Administration in its statistical work classifies an industry as "dominated by small business if at least 60 percent of the industry's employment is in firms with fewer than 500 employees." By that definition U.S. business on average is not mainly small-business–dominated, since firms with fewer than 500 employees accounted for 53 percent of paid employment in 1991. The only industry divisions meeting the small-business-dominated criterion were wholesale trade, retail trade, and construction. As might be expected, mining, manufacturing, transportation, and public utilities were the most dominated by large companies.

Measuring the size of firms, though, poses problems. For one thing, statistics for the very smallest firms—those with no paid employees—are nonexistent for some industry divisions and may not be of good quality in others, because it is common for many small businesses to understate their income—to judge from studies made by the Internal Revenue Service. For another, different measures of size can give different results, although within a narrowly defined industry that may not be a serious problem.

The use of employment to measure size can understate the importance of large companies, which have the funds to make investments in fixed capital. A more significant measure of size than employment is value added or national income produced. The chart illustrates the importance of the 200 biggest manufacturing firms when different size criteria are used.

PERCENTAGE OF FIRMS AND PERCENTAGE OF EMPLOYEES, BY SIZE OF FIRM, 1991

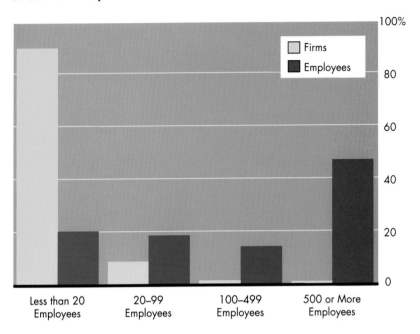

SHARES OF MANUFACTURING ACCOUNTED FOR BY THE 200 BIGGEST FIRMS, 1987

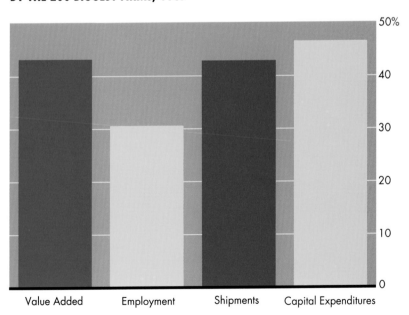

In manufacturing, there is
no evidence that
concentration of activity in
a small number of large
firms has increased in
recent decades.

Although a small number of very large firms dominate several U.S. industries, the U.S. economy does not appear to have become more concentrated than it was, say, in the mid-1970s. The share of value added accounted for by the 100 largest manufacturing companies rose from 23 to 33 percent between 1947 and 1963 but did not change over the next two and a half decades.

There are several problems with concentration ratios. While some firms continue to be ranked among the largest, in the top group turnover is frequent. Some firms that were household names a generation ago are scarcely known today. High concentration ratios were supposed to signify a lack of competition, a failure of markets. On the basis of the post–World War II experience, however, researchers have not been able to demonstrate a close connection between the degree of concentration and the existence of price flexibility. In addition, concentration figures have much less significance in an economy open to foreign competition than in a closed economy. The steel industry in the United States, for example, is still highly concentrated, but foreign competition has greatly altered its price behavior.

SHARES OF VALUE ADDED IN MANUFACTURING ACCOUNTED FOR BY THE BIGGEST FIRMS, 1947–1987

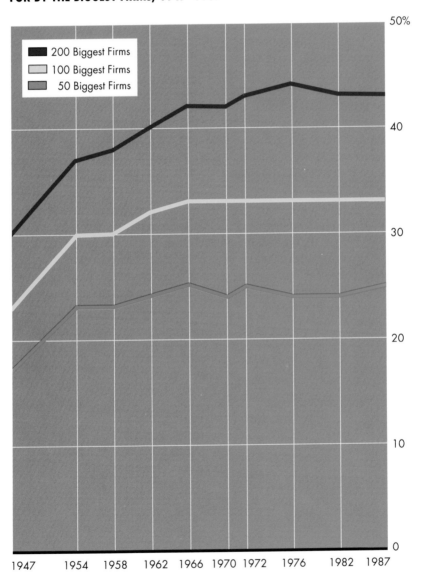

Outside of agriculture, the
number of self-employed
persons has been rising
since the late 1960s.
Except for the early depression
years, the number of self-
employed persons in farming—in addition to hired farm workers—has
declined continuously since the early part of this century, as farmers
found better-paying opportunities in nonfarm work. The number of self-
employed farmers in 1993—approximately 1 million—was about one-
fourth the number so classified in 1953.

Self-employed persons in nonfarm activities present a different picture. Their numbers also rose during the depression because jobs were
scarce. They rose again after World War II because demand was strong
and many veterans took advantage of the GI Bill to obtain government
loans to start new businesses. Most of these businesses, however, had
very short lives, and the number of self-employed fell gradually until some
time in the 1960s.

Since that time, the number of self-employed has increased markedly. Reasons for this movement are not clear, however. Conceivably, individuals who were formerly employees chose to become independent self-
employed contractors for reasons related to tax avoidance and perhaps
evasion. Increases in self-employment were especially large in finance
and real estate and in services, both of which also experienced large gains
in the number of employees in the 1970s and 1980s.

SELF-EMPLOYED PERSONS IN AGRICULTURAL AND NONAGRICULTURAL SECTORS, 1947–1993

MILLIONS OF PERSONS

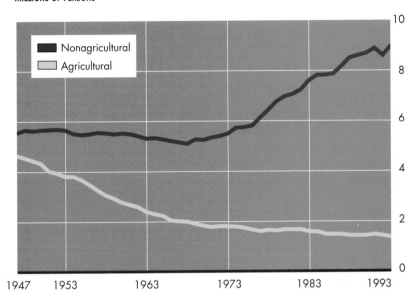

SELF-EMPLOYED PERSONS AS PERCENTAGE OF TOTAL EMPLOYMENT IN NONAGRICULTURAL SECTORS, 1947–1993

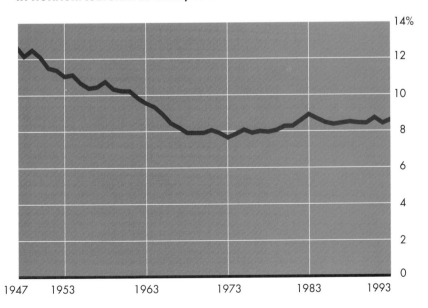

Large firms as well as small firms create new jobs. The basic question is, Which jobs have the longer life?

It has been said that small business creates most of the new jobs. Small firms indeed are constantly creating new jobs, mainly because hundreds of thousands of new businesses, most of them very small, are started each year. This kind of addition to employment is often referred to as "gross" job creation. The important question is, How permanent are these jobs? Experience shows that newly established firms have a very short life span, so that on balance the net contribution to employment, viewed over a long period, tends to be small. Large firms also create many new jobs, and since large firms tend to be well established, their new jobs tend to have greater permanence.

One way of looking at this is to examine census statistics on the share of employment accounted for by large and small firms over long periods. For manufacturing, this is illustrated in the chart. Small firms are represented by "single-unit" companies: those having only one place of business. In this example, large firms are equated with "multiunit" companies, those with more than a single place of business. Many of these multiunit firms are small, but the distinction is a useful one.

From 1929 to 1977 the share of manufacturing employment accounted for by single-unit companies declined, from 54.0 percent in 1929 to 23.6 percent in 1977. But since then it has risen somewhat. From 1947 to 1977, the declining share reflected absolute decreases in small firm employment and employment increases for large firms. From 1977 to 1987, however, the last year for which census data are available, employment in small firms increased, while employment in multiunit firms decreased. It is hard to say whether this reversal in the small firm share is temporary or whether it reflects a fundamental change in markets, possibly related to computer technology, which is favorable to small-scale organization. Downsizing by the largest firms was one of the features of the 1980s that continued in the 1990s, apparently at a slower pace.

Since the mid-1950s, the small-firm share in retail trade has fallen rapidly as chains have won increasing shares of the retail market and very small retailers have found it difficult to compete. Within the multiunit firm universe, however, local and regional chain supermarkets have achieved a dominant position, while national chains have lost market share.

SHARES OF MANUFACTURING EMPLOYMENT,
MULTIUNIT FIRMS VS. SINGLE-UNIT FIRMS, 1929–1987

% OF TOTAL EMPLOYEES

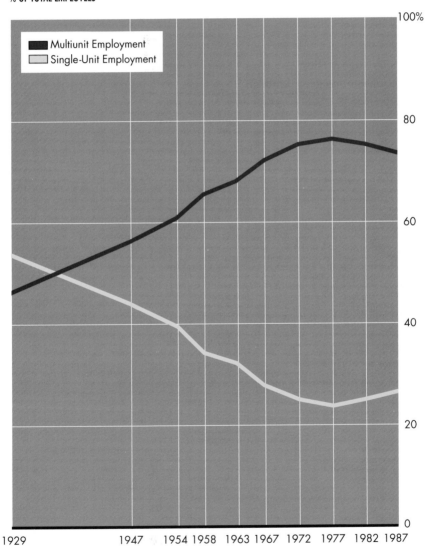

Legend:
- Multiunit Employment
- Single-Unit Employment

Most large U.S. industrial firms are multinational firms, with substantial operations in foreign countries.

Although this country did not "invent" the multinational corporation, setting up operations in foreign countries through direct investment has been characteristic of large American companies as far back as records go. In the early years especially, foreign investment did not come about because this country had large amounts of capital to invest abroad but because of what has been called "firm-specific assets"—production know-how, patents, and brand names that came from skills in marketing and advertising.

There are many ways of looking at multinational corporations. First, how important are parent companies in U.S. business? In 1989, the latest year for which production data are available, U.S. parent companies of U.S. multinationals had a GDP of more than $1 trillion, which represented 26 percent of U.S. business GDP excluding banks. In manufacturing, excluding petroleum, the parent company share was 61 percent; in petroleum, 88 percent; and in all other industries, 12½ percent. Parent shares have fallen when GDP is expressed in current dollars; parent companies contributed 32 percent of nonbank business GDP in 1977. The decline occurred mainly because multinationals are important in manufacturing and manufacturers' prices went up less than average from 1977 to 1989.

The $1 trillion associated with parent companies in 1989 would rise to almost $1.4 trillion when GDP of majority-owned foreign affiliates are accounted for. The GDP of the foreign affiliates was 23 percent of the $1.4 trillion. This share was not greatly different from the 25 percent share found in 1977. The 1977 share, however, was much higher than it was in 1957, to judge from employment data. So it appears that taken as a whole U.S. business reached a peak in its internationalization more than a quarter of a century ago. Strong growth in other industrialized countries and outward investment by large native firms in countries like Japan, Germany, and Sweden are the main reasons for the leveling in the U.S. share.

Two other recent findings of a Commerce Department study are worth noting. In relation to host countries, majority-owned foreign affiliates are small—5 percent or less of GDP in most countries and only 9 percent in Canada. Between 1977 and 1991, manufacturing multinational companies do not seem to have shifted to low-wage countries to any significant degree.

SHARES OF MULTINATIONAL CORPORATION GROSS PRODUCT, 1977, 1982, AND 1989

U.S. PARENTS AND MAJORITY-OWNED FOREIGN AFFILIATES

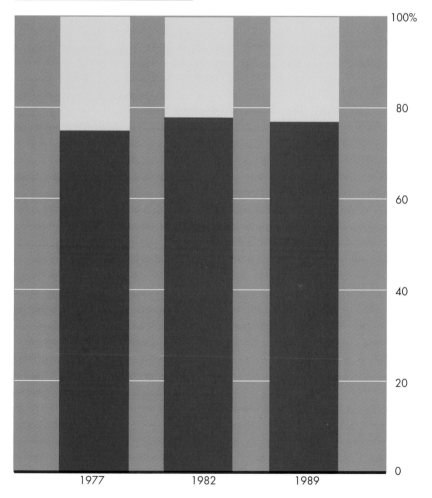

Union membership as a share of employment has declined since the 1950s.

Union membership grew in absolute numbers until about 1980 but has decreased since that time. The most rapid period of growth was in the late 1930s as a result of legislation that gave workers the right to organize. This period saw the rise of industrial unions.

As a share of employment or of the labor force, however, unionism peaked in the mid-1950s and has since undergone a steady decline. Several factors contributed to this trend. Unions had always had their greatest impact among blue-collar employees, but factory and related workers became less important as management substituted capital for labor. The 1950s and 1960s were a period of rapid growth in foreign investment by U.S. corporations. It is very likely that new competition from abroad made U.S. management less willing to recognize unions where that meant higher labor costs. The slowdown in the growth of productivity, which dates from the early 1970s, probably had similar effects. New legislation may have diminished the attractiveness of union membership. A law passed in 1974—the Employment Retirement Income Security Act (ERISA)—gave many workers pension rights that had previously been won through collective bargaining.

The absolute decline in union membership in the 1980s may have been influenced by the unsuccessful strike of the air traffic controllers, but the decline in the rate of inflation was very likely much more important. In a highly competitive environment, business found that it could not pass off wage increases in the form of price increases. "Givebacks" (wage reductions) became common; where increases were given, they were small, and plant closings and retrenchment in employment became the order of the day. In recent years the end of the cold war has had similar effects.

UNION MEMBERSHIP AS PERCENTAGE OF NONFARM EMPLOYMENT, 1930–1994

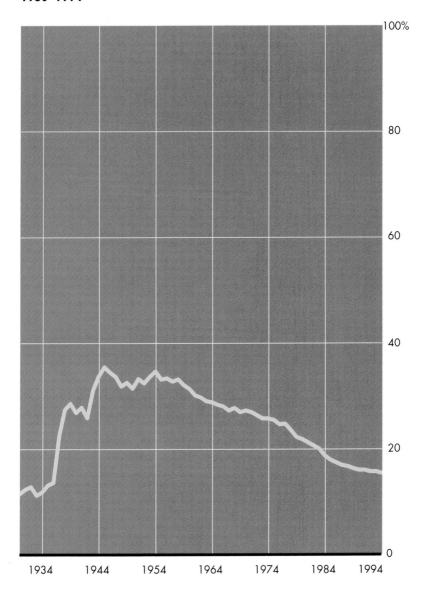

PART ELEVEN

Wealth and Debt

In 1992, 18 percent of American families owned stock, and another 11 percent owned mutual funds (not counting money market funds), according to a Federal Reserve study. The proportion of the population owning stocks directly has been growing since the early postwar period but not steadily, according to surveys run by the New York Stock Exchange. After the oil shock of 1973, stock prices fell and made only a partial recovery. The proportion of the population owning stocks declined during the period of uncertainty, but with the recovery of the market in the early 1980s that proportion resumed its rise.

Families that own stocks directly tend to have higher incomes, more wealth, and more education than the population at large. According to the 1992 Federal Reserve survey, about half the families with incomes of $100,000 or more owned stocks directly.

Because stocks are inherently risky, the proportion of the population owning stocks directly remains relatively low. Moreover, dislike of risk is probably a major reason for the changing composition of equity holdings. From 1965 to 1993, stock mutual funds held by households increased at an annual rate of 12.9 percent, as compared with a rise of 5.9 percent for corporate equities held by households directly. The growing popularity of mutual funds reflects among other things the desire of investors to diversify their holdings and thereby reduce risk.

PERCENTAGE OF FAMILIES OWNING STOCKS AND
MEDIAN VALUE OF HOLDINGS, BY FAMILY INCOME, 1992

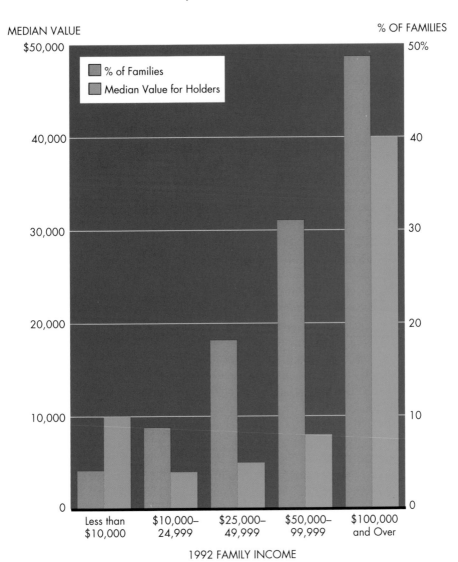

MEDIAN VALUE

% OF FAMILIES

- % of Families
- Median Value for Holders

1992 FAMILY INCOME

The value of stocks held by pension funds has grown much faster than the market value of all stocks. The growth of pension funds has greatly increased the number of Americans who own stocks indirectly.

The American people are the chief owners of American corporations, despite the highly publicized claims that foreigners are taking over U.S. businesses. The nature of that ownership has undergone a profound change in the post–World War II period. Up to a few decades ago, ownership in the hands of individuals and personal trusts represented middle-class and wealthy individuals. Today a new element in the picture is the pension fund, both private and state and local government. The beneficiaries of these funds are workers of all types—blue-collar as well as white-collar. Although these kinds of funds have been in existence a long time, their growth was extremely rapid from the late 1960s to the mid-1980s.

In 1948 the market value of stocks of domestic corporations was about $100 billion. Of this total, households held about 92 percent, and pension funds and insurance companies another 3 percent. The rest was held by foreign residents, stockbrokers, and others. At the end of 1993, the market value of equities had risen to $5.7 trillion. Although equities held by householders exceeded $3 trillion, this represented a considerably reduced household share, somewhat more than 50 percent. Private pension and state and local government funds plus insurance company holdings, however, rose to 30 percent. Holdings by foreign residents were less than 6 percent, while most of the remainder was in the hands of mutual funds and could be viewed as owned mainly by households.

In 1991, about 43 percent of civilian nonfarm wage and salary workers in this country reported that they participated in a pension plan. Although this figure would have to be reduced considerably to eliminate persons without "vesting" (persons not yet entitled to retirement benefits or lump-sum distributions) and although many pension funds do not have investments in corporate stocks, the number of indirect owners of stocks through these funds is very substantial. Further, in contrast to persons who own stocks directly, pension fund ownership is widely dispersed through a large part of the working population.

TOTAL VALUE OF CORPORATE EQUITIES AND HOLDINGS BY PENSION FUNDS AND INSURANCE COMPANIES, 1945–1993

BILLIONS OF $, LOGARITHMIC SCALE

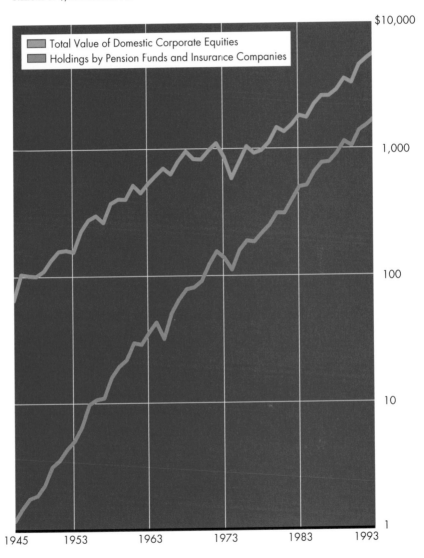

Although private debt has risen, private net worth—the excess of assets over liabilities—has increased at almost the same rate as GNP since the end of World War II.

The size of indebtedness in the United States is a common concern for three main reasons: (1) egregious examples in particular industries or regions where debt was undertaken on the basis of expectations that proved far too optimistic; (2) fears about the burden of the debt in the event of recession; (3) a strong aversion to debt held by many people. Debt has to be viewed in context, in relation to the assets behind the debt and to the ability of debtors to service the debt.

Net worth is the excess of assets over liabilities. According to Federal Reserve data, the consolidated private net worth of U.S. households, businesses, and nonprofit institutions at the end of 1993 was $22 trillion. Since 1946, private net worth has risen at an annual rate of 7.2 percent, not quite as much as the 7.5 percent average rise in GNP. Although the percentage growth in assets has been smaller than the rise in liabilities over this period, net worth has grown, because in the initial year there was a large excess of assets over liabilities. The assets embraced by this calculation are the tangible capital of private business, homes, consumer durables, and land plus what U.S. residents own in foreign countries net of what foreigners own here.

The data are subject to many qualifications. Land, for example, is valued at estimated current market price, while domestic assets other than land are valued at current costs. Putting a market value on any property, especially large and complex ones, is not easy. Current cost may or may not be an appropriate substitute.

PRIVATE NET WORTH AND CURRENT-DOLLAR GNP, 1945–1993

BILLIONS OF $, LOGARITHMIC SCALE

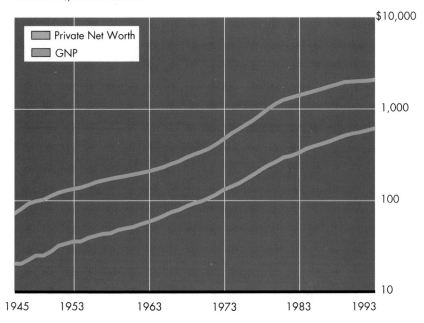

RATIO OF PRIVATE NET WORTH TO CURRENT-DOLLAR GNP, 1945–1993

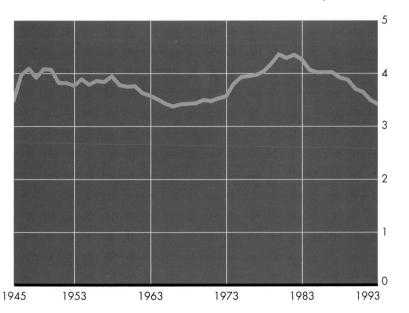

For much of the postwar period, the debt of nonfinancial corporations has been rising relative to what these companies produce.

Debt becomes burdensome during recessions, especially when downturns are deep and long lasting. During the 1982 recession, some analysts expressed fears either that the economy might not recover or that the recovery might be very slow because of the burden of the debt and the lack of liquidity. That fear proved to be unfounded. Similar concerns about excessive credit use and inadequate liquidity were expressed in the 1990–1991 recession, particularly in relation to the slow recovery of the economy in 1991 and 1992 in the face of a considerable easing of monetary policy. Determining when debt is "excessive" is a difficult task that economists and financial analysts often face. The charts illustrate two aspects of this problem for corporate business.

The first chart shows the ratio of credit market debt to GDP for nonfinancial corporations. Although this picture does not demonstrate that nonfinancial corporations as a whole took on an amount of debt that was excessive relative to corporate output, the ratios of 1989 and 1990 were somewhat high in relation to the postwar trend. These aggregates say nothing about particular industries or parts of the country. The real estate industry, especially commercial real estate, and the New England region went through well-publicized difficulties in the early 1990s. A few years earlier, the problems were concentrated in the oil-producing regions of the country.

Liquidity problems can become acute even for companies with substantial real assets if they have cash flow troubles. The second chart shows annual net interest payments relative to cash flow, where cash flow—undistributed profits plus depreciation—is calculated on the National Income and Product Accounts (NIPA) basis. The ratios in 1989 and 1990 were much higher than in the recession years of 1974 and 1982, but by 1993 they had fallen considerably.

CREDIT MARKET DEBT AS PERCENTAGE OF GDP FOR NONFINANCIAL CORPORATIONS, 1945–1993

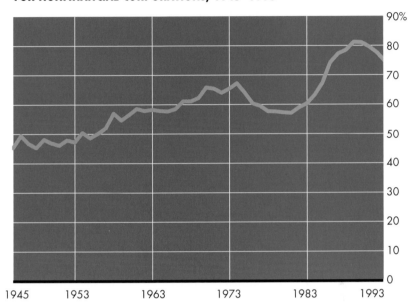

NET INTEREST AS PERCENTAGE OF CASH FLOW FOR NONFINANCIAL CORPORATIONS, 1945–1993

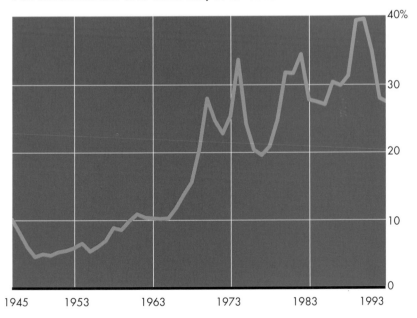

In the 1970s and 1980s, corporations increased their use of debt relative to equity for their external financing. A decline in the use of debt did not come until the 1990s.

In the postwar period, corporations have relied much more on debt than on equity for their external financing. Tax laws have encouraged debt financing because interest costs, unlike dividends, are a deductible expense, although reductions in the corporate tax rate in the 1980s should have lessened this influence.

One factor favoring debt financing is the rate of inflation. When the rate of inflation increased in the early 1970s, the incentive of corporations to invest in plant, equipment, and inventories was strengthened because business could borrow funds (from the household sector) at real rates of interest that were low and at times negative. In the 1960s, debt was only 41 percent of equity of nonfinancial corporations, but in the 1970s that percentage rose to 78.

Although high real interest rates and disinflation after the early 1980s should have brought about a large drop in the debt-equity ratio, the decline was not pronounced and a significant drop did not occur until the 1990s. Economists are not entirely clear about why debt financing was favored so much in the 1980s. Use of debt may have been encouraged by the emergence of various kinds of protective devices (hedging) in financial markets and by the increased internationalization of financial markets generally. More liberal bankruptcy laws in this country after 1979 as well as the spread of leveraged buyouts with junk bonds may also have affected this ratio.

RATIO OF DEBT TO EQUITY OUTSTANDING, NONFINANCIAL CORPORATIONS, 1945–1993

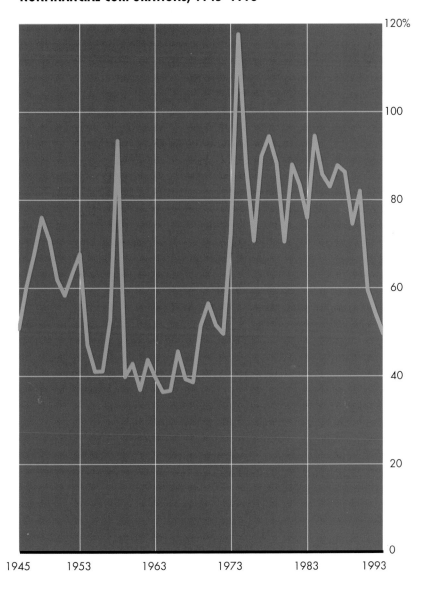

In 1991, half of U.S. households had a net worth of $36,600 or more. The ownership of wealth is highly concentrated.

The median net worth of households in 1991 was $36,600, according to the Census Bureau. Some 42 percent of that figure represented equity in home ownership (value of home less debt), about 14 percent was in interest-bearing accounts in financial institutions, and the rest was spread over various kinds of assets, like interest in a business or profession, other real estate, automobiles, individual retirement accounts, and Keogh accounts.

Wealth in the United States, as in most countries, tends to be very concentrated. The chart, covering 1992, is based on a Federal Reserve survey that pays special attention to families in the higher-income brackets. According to this survey, 27 percent of U.S. families had incomes of $50,000 or more and accounted for 70 percent of family net worth in that year. As compared with 1983, it appears that this group increased somewhat its percentage share of total family net worth, although from 1989 to 1992 the group with incomes of $100,000 or more experienced a decline in their share.

If households were ranked according to their wealth, the concentration would be more pronounced. Economists have estimated that the richest 1 percent of wealth holders held at least one-fourth of the total wealth in this country in the period 1922–1983. Over this sixty-year span, the share held by the top 1 percent declined.

Estimates of wealth distributions have a long history and at one time were based on estate tax returns filed by wealthier individuals. The traditional focus on wealthy persons' holding of stocks, bonds, real estate, and similar assets overlooks certain components of wealth owned by average families, like pension wealth and durable goods. As noted earlier, household durable goods constituted 12 percent of the entire domestic wealth of the United States including land in 1993.

Social security wealth, which is excluded from the foregoing statistics, is an important part of wealth that should be taken into account when measuring the level and trend of wealth and its concentration. Including the capitalized value of social security benefits would reduce the apparent concentration of wealth and accentuate its long-term decline. Inclusion of household durables and automobiles would also reduce wealth concentration.

DISTRIBUTION OF FAMILIES AND NET WORTH BY 1992 INCOME LEVEL

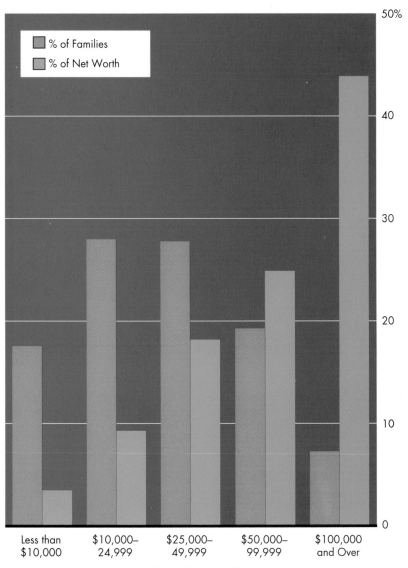

PART TWELVE

Economic Fluctuations

The U.S. economy, like other industrial economies, fluctuates around a rising long-term growth trend. There have been thirty cycles of expansion and contraction since 1854 and nine since the end of World War II.

The American economy, like other modern industrial economies, fluctuates around a rising trend. These fluctuations, generally referred to as "business cycles," have been documented in this country at least back to the middle of the nineteenth century. Concern over fluctuations—contractions because they bring unemployment and expansions because they lead to inflation—has been the dominant motif of national economic policy in much of the twentieth century.

The chart plots quarterly, seasonally adjusted data for an index of the so-called coincident indicators (as distinct from "leading indicators").

Economists distinguish different phases of economic fluctuations. Expansions are marked by increases in production, employment, and many other aspects of economic activity, but these tend to slow down and reach a peak. The peak is followed by decreases in production and employment and by rising unemployment until a bottom or trough is reached. Then the process starts all over again as the economy goes through a recovery phase and resumes another expansion, which continues until another peak is reached.

Lines of demarcation between these phases of the business cycle are often fuzzy, because the statistics are subject to all kinds of errors and often seem contradictory. Sometimes months may go by before it is generally recognized that a recession—or a recovery— is under way.

Theories about the causes of economic fluctuations abound. Some are related to the waves of optimism and pessimism that accompany the increases and decreases in economic activity. When sales are increasing, business spirits become buoyant, at times giving rise to beliefs that the expansion will continue indefinitely. Investments that look profitable at first turn out to be unprofitable when markets weaken. In this regard many economists assign a special role to the durable goods sector of the economy as the source of instability, because durable goods have long lives and their purchases can be postponed. There is no single explanation, however, of the business cycle, and the factors that may be important in one period are not necessarily the same as those in another.

QUARTERLY BUSINESS ACTIVITY, 1948–1994

INDEX: 1987 AVERAGE = 100; LOGARITHMIC SCALE

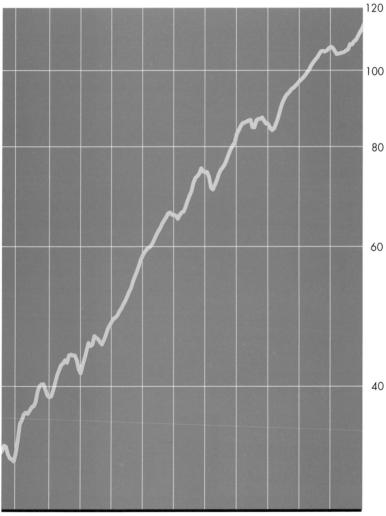

1950 1954 1958 1962 1966 1970 1974 1978 1982 1986 1990 1994

NOTE: Composite index of four coincident indicators.

The length of fluctuations
in the economy is highly
uneven, and there does
not seem to be any
"normal" duration. But
expansions are much
longer than contractions.

Expansions in the postwar period have been as short as 12 months and as long as 106 months and have averaged 45 months. The last full expansion—from November 1982 to July 1990—was very long by postwar standards. Contractions fall in a much narrower range: 6 to 16 months, with an average of 11 months. The most recent contraction—from July 1990 to March 1991—was a little shorter than average but was perceived differently because the upturn in its early stages was slower than average. The fact that expansions are four times as long as contractions is an aspect of long-term growth in the economy.

Fluctuations differ not only in duration but also in degree of change. The largest decline in real GDP in the post–World War II period was the 4.1 percent decline over the five quarters ending in the first quarter of 1975. The median decline has been a little over 2 percent. This irregularity in expansions and contractions introduces a good deal of uncertainty in business operations and is perhaps the main reason that governments and central banks have not been notably successful in getting rid of the business cycle. It is also an important reason for the rise of a large forecasting industry. Because expansions last a number of years, the typical forecaster, who attempts to look ahead for one year or possibly two, is more often right than wrong. But the record of economists in foreseeing "turning points"—dating the times when the economy will reach a peak or a trough—is not good.

LENGTH OF POSTWAR EXPANSIONS, 1945–1990

NUMBER OF MONTHS

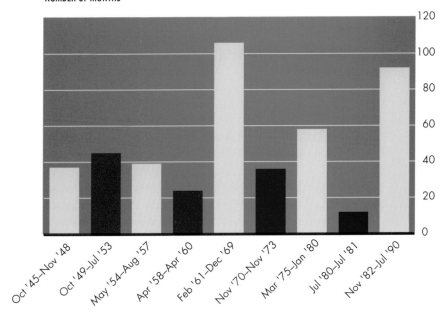

LENGTH OF POSTWAR CONTRACTIONS, 1948–1991

NUMBER OF MONTHS

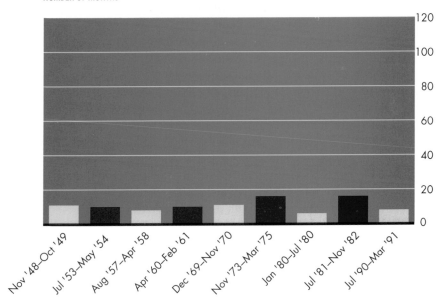

The 1929–1933 contraction was unique, as measured by the decline in output and employment and by the rise in unemployment.

The contraction of 1929–1933 lasted forty-three months, four times the length of the average post–World War II contraction. Real GNP in 1933 was some 28 percent below its 1929 level, in contrast with a median decline of 2.2 percent for the post–World War II contractions. Unemployment reached 25 percent in 1933.

Another common way of gauging recessions is to measure how much time elapses before the economy attains the output level it had at its previous peak. For the contractions since the end of World War II, that interval has averaged about a year and a half. With the Great Depression, however, it took ten years before real GNP got back to its 1929 level. Because the labor force kept growing and productivity increasing, unemployment was still very high in 1939: 17.2 percent versus an estimated 3.2 percent in 1929.

Only the huge rise in demand due to World War II eliminated the high unemployment of the 1930s. And after the war the economy did not slip back into its pre–World War II condition of high unemployment and idle capacity. Since the end of the war the economy has enjoyed reasonably full employment, interrupted by recessions of fairly brief duration and mixed experience with inflation.

The comparative mildness of postwar recessions is attributable to many factors. In comparison with the pre–World War II period, government is much more important in the economy. In 1929 total government purchases were only 14 percent of real GDP. Since 1945, they have never been less than 17 percent. The salient point is that government purchases tend to be independent of business downturns. A similar influence is the growth of government transfer payments, like social security, which continue regardless of business activity and, in the case of the unemployment insurance programs, expand when the economy declines. Transfers in 1994 were 17 percent of personal income; in 1929, less than 2 percent.

Modern governments with the help of central banks are committed to preventing very severe recessions. Because this policy is widely expected, it tends to limit drastic cuts in spending in the private sector. By the same token, modern economies may have an inflationary bias.

U.S. CIVILIAN UNEMPLOYMENT RATE, 1929–1993

PERCENT

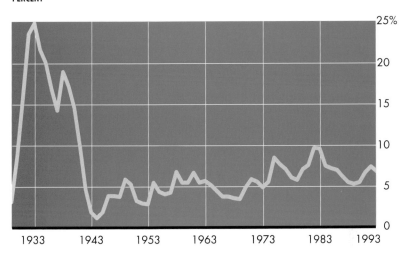

EMPLOYMENT CHANGES IN NONFARM ESTABLISHMENTS
DURING ECONOMIC CONTRACTIONS, 1929–1991

% CHANGE

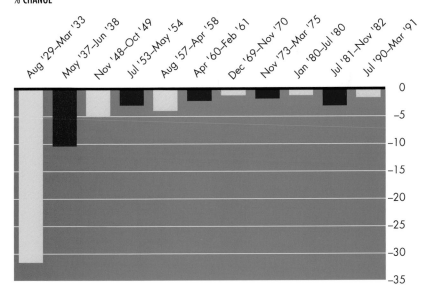

Although the causes of the Great Depression are uncertain, the big decline in the money supply was probably an important factor.

An enormous literature has grown up about the causes of the Great Depression, and while interest in that period has subsided, it has by no means disappeared. Many reasons have been given for the depression: the loss of confidence among businessmen and consumers because of the 1929 stock market crash and the bank failures of the early 1930s; the high tariffs passed by Congress in 1930; the maturing of the American economy and the decline in investment opportunities; and the perverseness of monetary policy.

Studies made by economists over the postwar years have emphasized the lack of economic understanding on the part of the government, the monetary authorities, and the politicians, as well as on the part of the economists of the time. President Hoover was baffled by the economic disaster that beset his administration. Franklin D. Roosevelt campaigned on a platform of a balanced budget. It did not take long, however, for the new administration to step up spending.

Most economists now agree that monetary policy was extremely poor. As a result of the research by economists Milton Friedman and Anna Schwartz, we now know that the Federal Reserve shrank the money supply instead of increasing it as a means of stemming the economic decline. From August 1929 to March 1933, the money stock fell by more than one-third. This was more than three times as much as the largest preceding declines—the reductions of 9 percent in 1875–1879 and again in 1920–1921. While a severe contraction in economic activity could probably not have been avoided, economists now believe that the decline would not have been so pronounced had the money supply not been reduced so much.

U.S. MONEY STOCK, 1914–1939

BILLIONS OF $

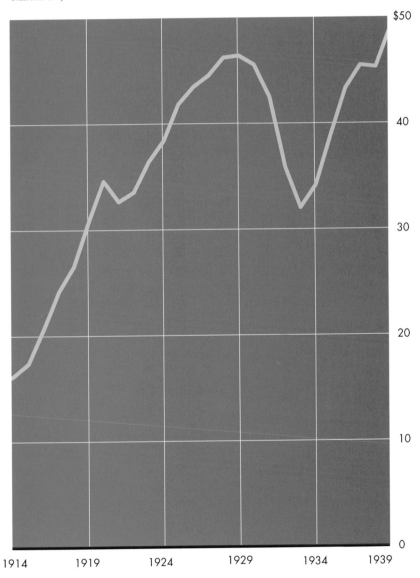

In 1994, 6.1 percent of the civilian labor force was unemployed. About 48 percent were persons who had lost their jobs.

The Current Population Survey (CPS) is used by the U.S. government to measure unemployment. It has been in existence since 1940, although it has been changed from time to time, the last major revision being in January 1994. The procedures started in 1940 for measuring unemployment were a great step forward. During the 1930s, when unemployment was very high, the public had to contend with several unemployment estimates that differed in both level and movement and were the source of continuing controversy.

The CPS was a genuine breakthrough in two respects: it made use of modern probability sampling methods in a monthly survey on a scale never before seen, and it introduced the concept of the labor force. The labor force is the sum of the number of persons employed and the number of persons unemployed; the unemployment rate is the number unemployed divided by the labor force. The labor-force concept is a simple one but even today is not well understood. Many people think that if employment goes up, unemployment must go down, but that is so only if the labor force is unchanged, and experience has demonstrated that the labor force is subject to much change.

To be classified as unemployed in the Current Population Survey, the individual must have had no work in the survey week; must have been available for work; and must have tried to find a job in the four-week period ending in the survey week. The unemployed include those who:

- have lost their jobs
- are entering the labor force for the first time
- are coming back to the labor force
- have quit their last job and are looking for another (see chart)

At the beginning of 1994, the BLS introduced a comprehensive overhaul of the CPS, the first since 1967. On the basis of an overlap survey, it was thought at the time that the new survey approach would raise the unemployment rate by an estimated six-tenths of 1 percent over the rate that would have been obtained with the old procedures. But that figure has now been reduced to two-tenths, half of which reflects new weights based on the 1990 Population Census. Starting in 1994, the figures are not strictly comparable with previously published numbers.

PERCENTAGE DISTRIBUTION OF UNEMPLOYED, 1994

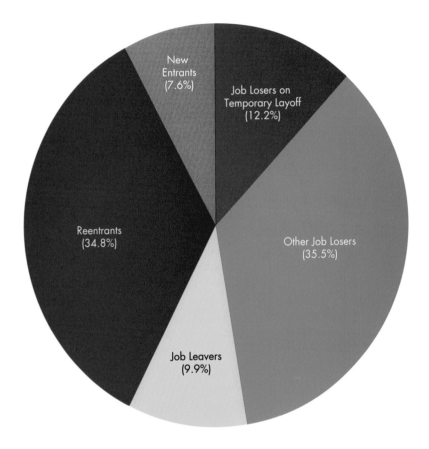

Since the late 1960s, the median duration of unemployment has averaged six and a half weeks. It was 9.2 weeks in 1994.

Most unemployment is of short duration. Even in 1982, when unemployment was higher than in any other postwar year, 36 percent of the unemployed were out of work for spells of less than five weeks. The average (mean) duration of unemployment reached its postwar peak of twenty weeks in 1983, but even then half the unemployed had been out of work for ten weeks or less (the median duration of unemployment). In 1994, when the average duration was 18.8 weeks, half the unemployed had been out of work for less than 9.2 weeks (the median).

As the top chart indicates, the mean length of unemployment has increased over the postwar years. One aspect of this is the proportion of the unemployed who have experienced very long spells of unemployment. In the 1950s, less than 10 percent of the unemployed had spells lasting more than six months, but in the 1980s the proportion rose to 15 percent. This sharp increase in the long-term proportion is probably related to structural changes in the economy, like the one associated with the oil shock at the end of 1973 and the cutbacks in defense production associated with the end of the cold war.

The duration statistics themselves are subject to two biases that operate in different directions. As a random sample of households, they are more likely to pick up an individual who has had a long spell of unemployment than a person who was unemployed only briefly, say, a few weeks. In contrast, a person who reports that he has been unemployed for a given number of weeks is describing a condition that has not been completed.

DURATION OF UNEMPLOYMENT, IN WEEKS, 1948–1994

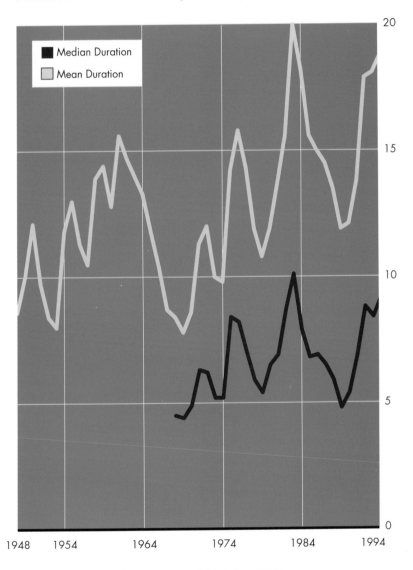

NOTE: Data for the median are not available before 1968.

The burden of unemployment is much heavier among those families that have children and are headed by women.

The individual is the main focus of the statistics on employment and unemployment in the Current Population Survey. It makes a difference, though, if the unemployed individual is, for example, a young person looking for summer work or an adult who is the chief support of a family. How much of a hardship unemployment represents is better measured by looking at families.

The Labor Department reported that in 1993, when the unemployment rate was 6.8 percent, 9.2 percent of all families experienced some unemployment. Of these, 30 percent had no family member employed during the year. If the family had children under eighteen years of age, the proportion rose to 34 percent. If these numbers are looked at a different way, for all families experiencing unemployment, with or without children, 70 percent had at least one person working. The proportion dropped to 62 percent if employment is limited to full-time (rather than part-time) work. The figures cited above look somewhat better than average for white families, much worse than average for black families, and about average for Hispanic families.

In 1993 more than three-quarters of all families were married-couple families; of these, 8 percent experienced unemployment. Not surprisingly, among this group of unemployed a smaller than average proportion—19 percent—had no family member employed. Whether the married couples were white, black, or Hispanic made little difference. What is strikingly different, however, is the importance of married couples in all families. Among blacks, married-couple families were only 45 percent of all families; among whites the 1993 proportion was 82 percent.

When the focus shifts to families headed by women, the picture looks much worse. This type of family was 18 percent of all families in 1993. For this group, the unemployment rate was 12 percent. Among the unemployed, 56 percent had no employed person in the family in 1993. The proportions were somewhat better than average for whites, poorer for blacks, and about average for persons of Hispanic origin. But whereas female-headed families were 14 percent of all white families, they were 50 percent of all black families and 24 percent of Hispanic.

PERCENTAGE OF FAMILIES WITH SOME UNEMPLOYMENT WITH NO EMPLOYED PERSON DURING 1993

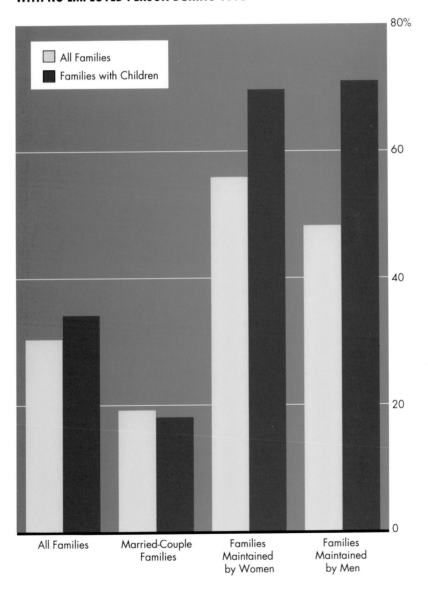

Despite increases in the past several years, white-collar unemployment rates are still below blue-collar rates.

Throughout American history, the introduction of new labor-saving technologies has been accompanied by deep concern that the new technology would bring about a large rise in unemployment. The record since 1940, when official unemployment measures started, does show a rise in the civilian unemployment rate, but it is by no means clear that this is a consequence of technological change. Estimates of unemployment for the twentieth century before 1940 made by Stanley Lebergott portray a rather flat picture (by decades) until the Great Depression.

The 1960s saw great concern over automation, which was the first application of computer technology to industrial processes. There can be little doubt that throughout the post–World War II period the introduction of all kinds of labor-saving devices has held down the demand for blue-collar workers. At its peak in 1979, employment of "production workers"—the blue-collar core of factory employees—was only one-sixth higher than it was in 1948, even though all private nonfarm employment was 88 percent higher over the same period. The 1980s were especially difficult for factory labor, with employment down and blue-collar unemployment rates sharply higher, especially in the early part of the decade. Blue-collar unemployment rates in the 1990–1991 recession, however, were not as high as they were in the early 1980s.

White-collar unemployment rates have always been much lower than blue-collar rates. Both types rose from the 1960s to the 1970s to the 1980s, but a difference has shown up in the 1990s (through 1993). White-collar rates have risen in the 1990s, whereas blue-collar rates have declined in spite of the recession. Defense cutbacks and "restructuring" by large companies are mainly responsible for this latest development. Recent white-collar rates, however, are still well below blue-collar rates.

UNEMPLOYMENT RATES BY OCCUPATION, 1958–1993

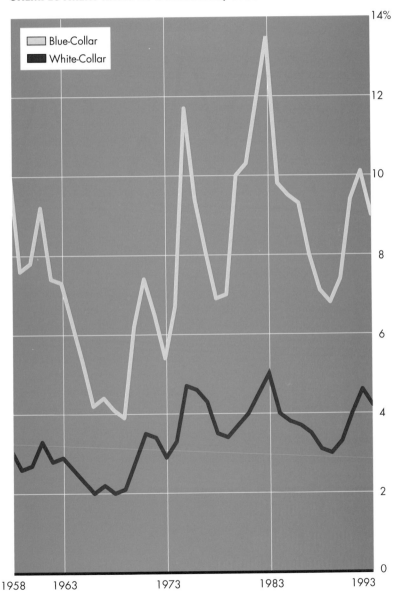

A fairly large proportion
of the labor force
experiences some
unemployment during
any year.

The results of the monthly unemployment survey have been likened to a snapshot. The snapshot records, for the survey week of each month, persons working and persons looking for work. Those who had looked for work in the past but decided to stop in the survey week and those who intended to seek work at a later date but had not begun their search as of the survey week do not appear in the labor-force statistics of that month. Generally speaking, only those who worked or were still looking for work are counted as part of the labor force. Ordinarily, persons who did not seek work in the survey week are excluded from the labor force.

Brief spells of unemployment are fairly common in the U.S. labor market. In the past two decades, the annual rate of unemployment was lowest in 1989, at 5.3 percent. In that year persons experiencing some unemployment were 12.9 percent of the number of persons who either worked or looked for work. (Persons who either worked or looked for work at any time during the year constitute a somewhat larger number than the civilian labor force.) More than 90 percent of those who experienced some unemployment during the year also worked at some time during the year. In 1993, the latest year for which data are available, the official unemployment rate of 6.8 percent was accompanied by a figure of 14.8 percent for those persons experiencing some unemployment; 83 percent of those with unemployment in 1993 worked at some point during the year. The 1993 experience is not strictly comparable with 1989 because 1989 was at the top of a business cycle expansion, whereas 1993 was at an early phase of the expansion. In 1982, the year of the highest unemployment rate in the postwar period (9.7 percent), persons experiencing some unemployment were 22 percent of the total who worked or looked for work.

PERCENTAGE OF PERSONS WITH SOME UNEMPLOYMENT
AND THE UNEMPLOYMENT RATE, 1958–1993

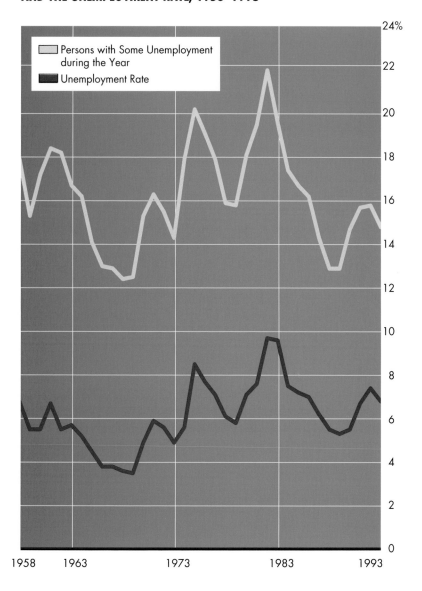

The level of unemployment rose from the 1950s to the 1980s, for reasons that are not entirely clear.

Economists do not have a good understanding of the long-term rise in the unemployment rate that the United States has experienced in the postwar period. Certainly, part of the reason for the rise shown in the chart is cyclical. Both the 1970s and the 1980s contained a more serious recession than did the 1950s or 1960s.

Still, it is clear that the unemployment rate in prosperous years is now higher than it was in prosperous years in the 1950s and 1960s. Twenty years ago economists thought that the changing age and sex composition of the labor force could explain much of the rise. In the early 1970s to a greater extent than in the early postwar period, the labor force consisted of young people and women, who typically had higher unemployment rates than adult men. But changes in the labor market in the 1990s have weakened that explanation.

Another hypothesis is that the spread of income support programs like unemployment insurance and welfare have made people less willing to work at the available wage. Still another possibility is that the growth of two-earner families makes the unemployment of one earner less of a burden and thus permits longer searching for a suitable job. One cannot rule out differences in the intensity of demand. In the 1950s this country was still recovering from the effects of the depression and the war.

The low unemployment of the 1950s and 1960s was noteworthy because it was accompanied by comparatively low inflation. This favorable combination may have come about because both business and labor had low inflationary expectations; memories of the Great Depression, with its high unemployment and low wages and prices, were still strong. Perhaps it should not be surprising that as those memories and the attitudes they gave rise to faded, the notion of a full-employment economy was taken for granted by labor and business, who believed that costs could be increased and prices raised with no adverse effect on employment and unemployment.

In the mid-1990s, the possibility existed that a better combination of low unemployment and low inflation might be regained, as a result of experience with lower inflation rates, stronger international competition, and a decline in the power of trade unions.

CIVILIAN UNEMPLOYMENT RATE BY DECADE, 1950s–1990s

PERCENT

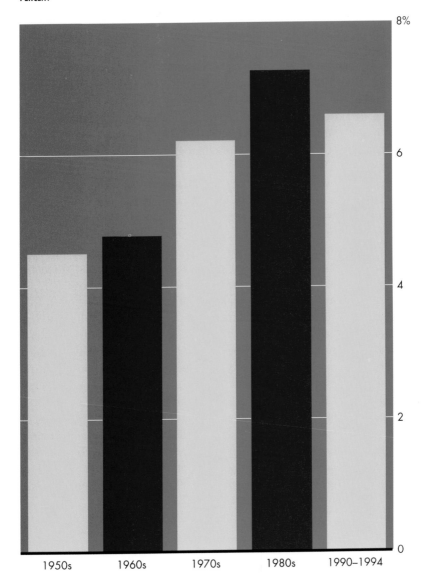

For several years the unemployment rate in the United States has been lower than rates in other major countries.

In recent years unemployment rates in the major industrialized countries—except for Japan—have been much higher than in this country. In 1993, for example, when the U.S. rate was 6.8 percent, rates were above 10 percent in France, Italy, the United Kingdom, and Canada. This was not always the case. In the ten years from 1974 to 1983, which embraced the two oil shocks, the U.S. unemployment rate was above that of the other major OECD countries except for Canada. In the following decade, however, the U.S. rate fell while the rate abroad rose (see chart). From 1983 to 1993, civilian employment rose 18 percent in this country, as compared with a median gain of 8 percent for the six other large OECD countries.

The usual explanation for the changed unemployment situation concerns differences in labor markets. Where the United States has relatively free markets in which businesses and labor can move with ease, foreign countries are hampered by high wages and restrictive labor practices. This country used to be the country with the highest wages in manufacturing, but that has not been true for some time. Social benefits abroad are maintained at a high level, as are the taxes required to finance them.

A recent study by McKinsey and Company takes issue with this explanation. According to this study, the fault is to be found not in the operation of labor markets but in the operation of product markets. Businesses abroad are hampered by restrictive regulations that make innovations difficult. For example, in many European countries the hours during which stores are open are limited by law, and as a consequence large-scale, lower-cost retail operations are discouraged.

European integration is attempting to modify restrictive practices of all kinds, but the imposition of uniform standards may make adjustments more difficult to bring about. Countries may find it difficult to make the choices about wages, working conditions, and social benefits as well as about the working of product markets that will avoid higher unemployment.

UNEMPLOYMENT RATES BY COUNTRY, 1974–1983 AND 1984–1993

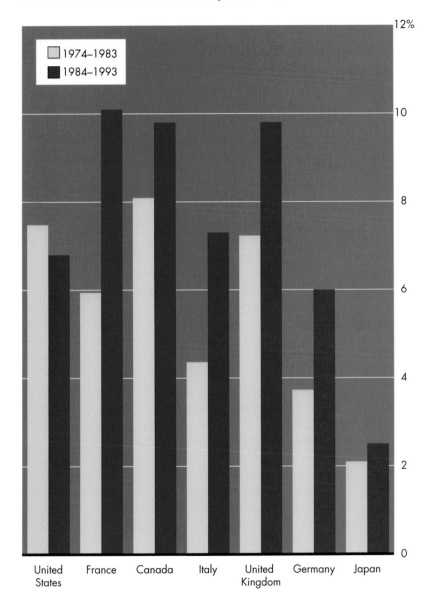

Before World War II, inflation was unusual in the United States, except in wartime. Since World War II, inflation has continued, even in peacetime.

After the big inflations of the Civil War and World War I, the United States entered prolonged periods in which the price level fluctuated along a declining trend. This trend eliminated most of the increase in the general price level that had occurred during the wars. By 1916, the consumer price index (CPI) was only 21 percent higher than it had been in 1860, at the beginning of the Civil War. For the whole fifty-six-year period, including the war, the annual rate of increase of the CPI was only three-tenths of 1 percent.

In 1940 the CPI was only 28 percent higher than in 1916, before the United States entered World War I. In that twenty-four–year period, the average inflation rate was 1 percent a year.

The rate of inflation surged during the period of World War II and the Korean War and again during the years of the Vietnam War and the two oil shocks. These surges, though, were not followed by years of a declining price level. Even in the relatively calm period from 1982 to 1994, the annual increase of the CPI averaged 3.6 percent.

One reason for the difference in behavior between the period before 1940 and the period since may have been a difference in the composition of output. In the earlier period, the kinds of products, mainly food, whose prices are very flexibly determined in highly competitive markets were more important in the market basket than they became later. Another reason may have been the increased commitment of government policy after the depression of the 1930s to use all its powers to prevent any increase in unemployment. This policy may have led to the expectation that the price level would never go down again but would have a permanently rising trend.

The figures here may overstate the degree of the change in price-level behavior somewhat. Output today contains more sophisticated and complex products, whose quality is difficult to measure, than formerly. The measurement of changes in the price level probably underestimates recent improvements in the quality of products and therefore overestimates the rate of inflation more than in earlier periods. But to the extent that is so, it is surely not the whole story.

CHANGE IN CONSUMER PRICE INDEX, 1860–1994

ANNUAL RATE, % CHANGE

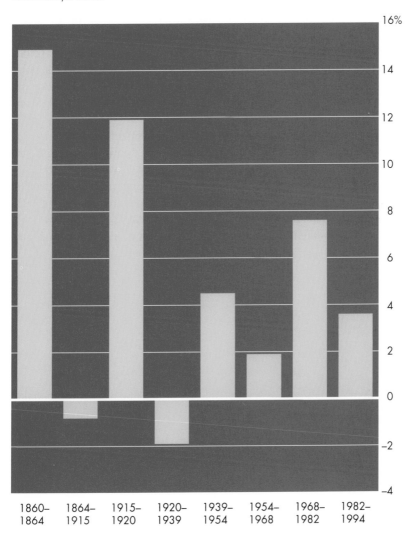

| 1860–
1864 | 1864–
1915 | 1915–
1920 | 1920–
1939 | 1939–
1954 | 1954–
1968 | 1968–
1982 | 1982–
1994 |

NOTE: Lengths of intervals differ.

The rate of inflation has fluctuated widely from year to year in the postwar period. Much of America's postwar economic history can be seen in the chart, which shows the annual change in the Consumer Price Index. The big peaks came in 1974–1975 and 1979–1981, at the time of the sharp increases in oil prices. The oil price increases of these years were quickly transmitted into the rest of the price system, so that an index of prices excluding energy products also peaks at the same time. A lower peak came in 1951, with the beginning of the Korean War. The effects of the Vietnam War and of the economic expansions of 1957 and 1989–1990 are also visible.

Recent evidence that the CPI somewhat overstates the true rate of inflation in the long run probably means that the figures shown here are a little higher than they should be. That would, not, however, alter the picture of the year-to-year fluctuations because the long-run overstatements, as far as is known, are fairly smoothly distributed from year to year. But it may also be true that the price indexes understate price increases in a boom and overstate them in a recession, so that cyclical fluctuations are understated.

ANNUAL PERCENTAGE CHANGE IN THE CPI, 1949–1994

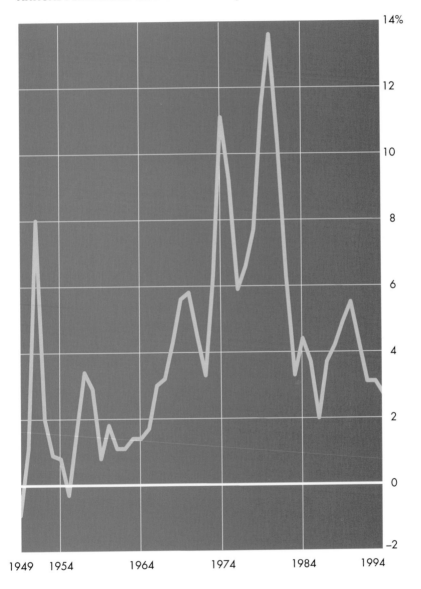

Monetary policy has substantial effects on the economy.

Monetary policy is a major instrument the government uses in an effort to stabilize the economy. The influence of monetary policy—control of the money supply—is derived from the fact that at any time people want to hold a certain amount of money in relation to their income. If the money supply exceeds what people want to hold, they will use it to increase their purchases or investments, which will raise total expenditures in the economy and raise total output or the price level or both. Conversely, if the money supply is less than they want to hold, their response will depress output or the price level.

The problem with managing the money supply so as to stabilize the economy lies in two conditions:

• An uncertain amount of time will elapse before a decision to change the money supply will result in an actual change and the effect is felt in the economy.

• How much money people will want to hold at a time in the future is not predictable within a certain margin of error.

It is possible, then, that a decision to change the money supply that seems entirely appropriate to the state of the economy at the time may be quite inappropriate when the decision takes effect. If, for example, the economy is depressed, an increase in the money supply may seem appropriate, but by the time that increase takes effect, people may have reduced the amount of money they want to hold—perhaps because they have become more optimistic about future conditions—so that the increase in the money supply turns out to be unexpectedly inflationary.

Despite this difficulty, some gross conclusions about monetary policy are probably valid:

• Extreme inflations—like that experienced in the United States during the Civil War or in Latin America and Israel in the 1980s—do not occur without very rapid rates of growth of the money supply.

• Even more moderate inflations cannot continue for a long time without persistently high monetary growth. The chart shows the rough but unmistakable relation between changes in the price level over twenty-year spans and changes in the money supply over the same periods since 1869.

• Major declines in the supply of money are likely to cause serious depressions—as was seen in 1929–1933.

MONEY AND PRICES IN THE LONG RUN, 1889–1993

% CHANGES OVER TWENTY-YEAR SPANS, ANNUAL RATES

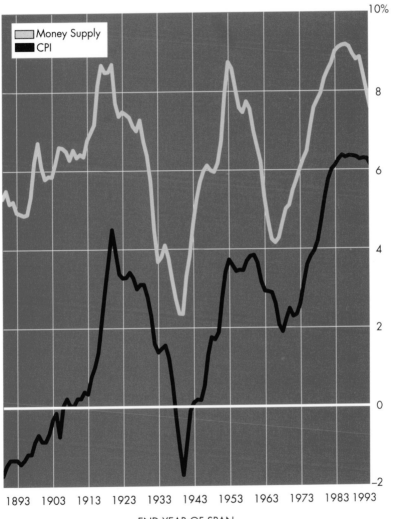

END YEAR OF SPAN

NOTE: Money supply approximates M2.

Management of monetary
policy in the short run
encounters many
difficulties. The difficulty of managing monetary policy arises mainly in con-
nection with the ordinary cyclical fluctuations of output and the price
level.

The chart suggests both the possibility of stabilizing the economy by
the use of monetary policy and the difficulty of doing so. From about 1960
to 1973, there was a fairly close relation between the rate of increase of
the money supply and the rate of inflation. (The chart compares the rate
of increase of the money supply with the change in the price level two
years later.)

But for a while after 1981, the rate of inflation subsided, while the
rate of monetary expansion increased. Then in 1985 the rate of inflation
began to rise again, but moderately, while monetary expansion abated but
remained fairly high. It appeared that during much of this period, if the
Federal Reserve had pursued what ordinarily would have been considered an anti-inflationary monetary policy, the result would have been to
depress the economy unduly. The continuing decline in the rate of monetary growth was then followed by what would have been regarded as a
more ordinary decline in the inflation rate from 1991 to 1994. This brief
experience did not, however, establish confidence in the ability to stabilize the economy or the price level within narrow limits.

Various strategies have been proposed for managing monetary policy in the face of its short-run uncertainties:
- stabilization of a particular price—usually gold
- stabilization of the rate of growth of the money supply, somehow
defined
- "feed-back" rules that would make the money supply respond
automatically and promptly to observed changes in economic conditions
- stabilization of interest rates
- discretionary adjustment of the money supply to the state of the
economy as appraised by the Federal Reserve
- discretionary adjustment of interest rates

On the whole, monetary authorities have preferred discretionary
strategies. At the end of 1994, the dominant strategy of the Federal
Reserve was to decide from time to time on the short-run interest rate
that it thought, having weighed all available evidence, was most likely to
yield the desired behavior of the economy.

THREE-YEAR CHANGES IN MONEY AND PRICES, 1962–1992

ANNUAL RATE OF CHANGE

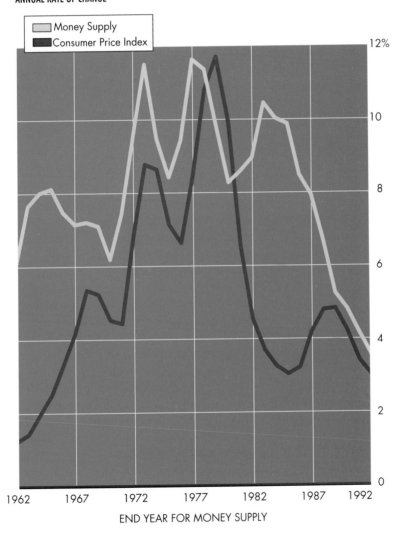

NOTE: Three-year increase in money supply is compared with three-year increase of CPI two years later. Money supply is M2.

There is uncertainty
about which assets
should be considered
"money."

As explained earlier, among all the kinds of assets the public holds, something called "money" is singled out for particular attention because a special relation is believed to exist between that asset and the public's total income or expenditures.

To serve the purposes of economic analysis and monetary policy, we want to identify a class of assets that, first, has the necessary stable relation to incomes and expenditures and, second, can be controlled by the monetary authority. The class of assets that best meets these tests is not constant but changes with economic practice and the availability of various financial instruments. Probably for a long time "money" could be identified with currency, as the asset used in transactions and as the most secure and liquid store of value. At a later date the most useful definition of money was currency plus demand deposits, now known as M1. More recently, with the enormous growth of money market deposit accounts, time deposits, and money market mutual funds, on which people could readily draw, attention focused on a total, M2, that included them along with currency and demand deposits. Yet another definition of money, M3, adds to M2 certain classes of assets held mainly by financial institutions rather than the public. A still larger total, called L, for liquid assets, adds mainly Treasury bills and high-quality, short-term notes of businesses.

Which of these, or some other, classes of assets should be called "money" is an empirical matter, depending on which best meets the requirements of explanation, forecasting, and control for which the concept is used. Until recently, M2 was commonly accepted as the most useful single concept, but the answer is now regarded as highly uncertain. (Official data on M2 as now defined are available only from 1959 on. The longer money supply figures used in the charts on pages 175 and 195 are approximations to M2 derived from Friedman and Schwartz, *Monetary Trends in the United States and the United Kingdom*, 1982, updated in the case of page 195 by the official M2 figures with minor adjustments.)

TYPES OF MONEY, DECEMBER 1960 AND DECEMBER 1994

BILLIONS OF $

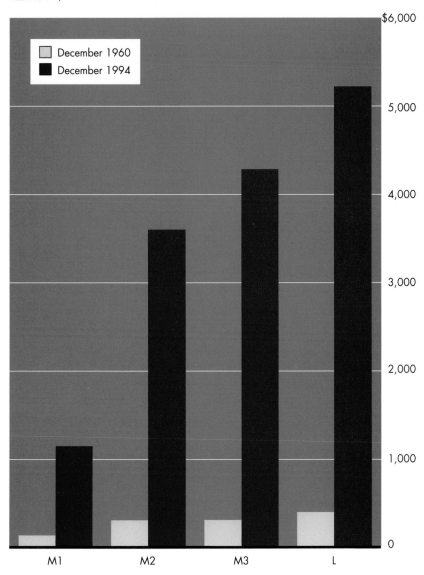

PART THIRTEEN

Government Expenditures, Taxes, and Deficits

Government expenditures are now about fourteen times as high, in real terms, as they were before the Great Depression. They are almost seven times as high per person and over twice as high as a percentage of GDP.

The charts refer to the total of federal, state, and local expenditures and include transfer payments and interest as well as purchases of goods and services. The big increase in expenditures as a percentage of GDP occurred between 1929 and 1949, when the ratio almost doubled, from 15 percent to 29 percent. That increase resulted from the new programs adopted during the New Deal, and even more from the aftermath of World War II, in the form of higher expenditures for defense, for veterans' benefits, and for interest on the war debt.

Since 1949 the ratio has varied within a 29 percent to 35 percent range. It rose toward the top of that range during the Korean War, the Vietnam War, and the defense buildup of the 1980s and fell after the Korean and Vietnam Wars. Aside from those three episodes, the trend of defense spending was downward, relative to GDP. At the same time, there was a rising trend of nondefense spending, especially for social security and Medicare and later for interest, relative to GDP. Since 1987, when defense spending as a share of GDP was falling to a sixty-year low, the rise of other expenditures has kept the total nearly constant.

Since the end of World War II, total and per capita real GDP have risen greatly, and that has permitted real government expenditures, total and per capita, also to rise sharply without breaking out of the 30 to 35 percent range as a share of GDP.

TOTAL GOVERNMENT EXPENDITURES IN 1987 DOLLARS, 1929–1994

INDEXES: 1929=100

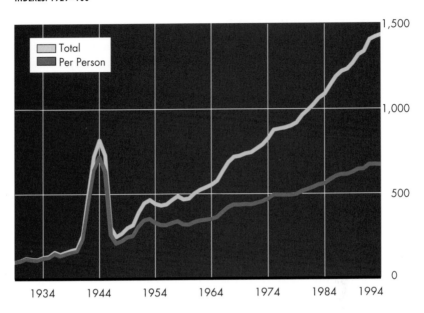

TOTAL GOVERNMENT EXPENDITURES
AS PERCENTAGE OF GDP, 1929–1994

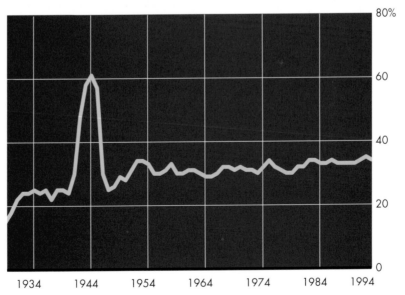

Before the Great Depression, state and local expenditures were much larger than federal expenditures, but since 1939 that situation has been reversed.

In 1929 state and local expenditures were about three times as large as federal expenditures. During the New Deal, the relative size of the federal government grew, as it assumed responsibility for relief and recovery from the depression. In 1934 and 1935, much of the increase of federal expenditure took the form of grants to states and localities to carry on relief and employment programs, but in the later part of the New Deal the increases were mainly for direct federal expenditures. This was also a time of some buildup of defense spending that, although tiny by our later experience, was still large relative to the budgets of that period.

The dominance of the federal sector since World War II has been due in part to the increased relative size of functions that have always been federal, mainly defense and interest on the federal government's debt. But it has also been due to the rapid growth of expenditures in fields the federal government did not formerly occupy, notably social security and health care.

Part of the expenditures made by state and local governments are financed by grants from the federal government. If these are considered expenditures of the federal government, the federal share in 1994 was about 68 percent; if they are considered state and local expenditures, the federal share was about 60 percent.

State and local expenditures for the purchase of goods and services—mainly for the pay of employees—are still much larger than those of the federal government. The federal lead is in transfer payments and interest. The number of state and local employees is about $3\frac{1}{2}$ times the number of federal employees, including the armed forces.

Although total state and local expenditures have declined markedly relative to federal expenditures, they remain about as high relative to the GDP as they were in 1929, about 11 percent if only expenditures from their own resources are counted.

FEDERAL EXPENDITURES AS PERCENTAGE OF TOTAL FEDERAL, STATE, AND LOCAL EXPENDITURES, 1929–1994

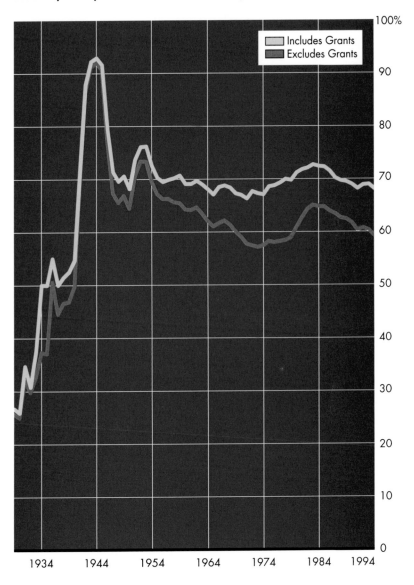

Defense spending in 1994 was lower, as a percentage of GDP, than in any year since the 1920s.

At the height of World War II, defense spending amounted to 40 percent of the GDP. In the postwar demobilization in the late 1940s it fell to about 6½ percent. With the Korean War, the ratio surged to 17½ percent. Since then it has fallen, with brief interruptions for the Vietnam War and the buildup during the Reagan administration, to 4.2 percent in 1994.

Although the percentage of the GDP going to defense was declining, the absolute amount of defense spending, in real terms, reached its peak in 1987, when it was higher than in the highest years of the Korean or Vietnam Wars. Since 1987 absolute spending has declined by almost one-quarter.

DEFENSE SPENDING AS PERCENTAGE OF GDP, 1947–1994

1947   1954   1964   1974   1984   1994

U.S. DEFENSE SPENDING, 1947–1994

BILLIONS OF $1987

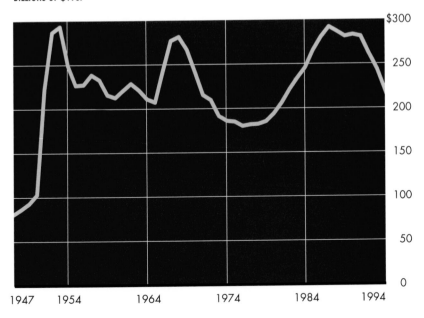

1947   1954   1964   1974   1984   1994

Foreign aid now accounts for about 1 percent of total federal expenditures.

This small item deserves recognition in a survey of the U.S. economy only because an exaggerated impression of the size of foreign aid expenditures in the federal budget is common. Thus one frequently hears suggestions that cutting foreign aid would be a practical way to eliminate, or at least substantially reduce, the federal deficit. In fact, in 1994 foreign aid was about 1 percent of total federal expenditures or $6\frac{1}{2}$ percent of the deficit.

Beginning in 1947, the chart shows expenditures for "international affairs," of which foreign aid is the largest component but which also includes the operation of the State Department and some other items. Expenditures for foreign aid separately, which are not available on a comparable basis before 1962, are also shown beginning in that year.

The high figures for 1947 to 1951 reflect the Marshall Plan. Since then, the fraction of total outlays devoted to foreign aid has been small and generally declining. In real terms, expenditures for "international affairs" are less than half as large as at their peak in 1949, and expenditures for foreign aid are one-fourth lower than in 1962.

At present, U.S. aid is directed primarily to countries in which the United States has a large political and security interest. The main recipients are Israel and Egypt.

U.S. EXPENDITURES FOR FOREIGN AID
AS PERCENTAGE OF FEDERAL EXPENDITURES, 1947–1994

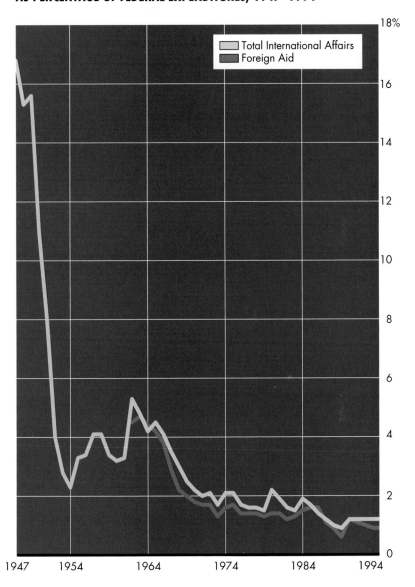

The rise of nondefense spending has been dominated by expenditures for health, income support, and education.

Between 1959 and 1992, total government nondefense expenditures (federal, state, and local), as a share of GDP, increased by almost three-quarters, from 17.3 percent to 29.9 percent. About three-quarters of this increase in the share was for three main functions—health, income support, and education. Expenditures for these functions rose from 55 percent of total nondefense expenditures in 1959 to 65 percent in 1992. The big increases in health and income support were at the federal level, especially if federal grants to states and localities for those purposes are considered federal expenditures.

The increase for health was primarily for Medicare, although Medicaid was also a significant factor. The increase for income support was mainly for social security. These two categories, health and income support, accounted for over 80 percent of the increase in federal nondefense expenditures as a share of GDP. Together with interest, they account for all (99 percent) of the increase in the federal nondefense share. Federal expenditures for education, even including grants, remained small, relative to GDP or to total government expenditures for education.

Interest expenditures more than doubled, all of that at the federal level, resulting from the increase in the federal debt and in rates of interest.

Expenditures for all functions other than those mentioned above, which include the provision of civil safety, roads and other transportation facilities, and the operation of the government, rose slightly more than the GDP, from 6.5 percent of GDP to 7.2 percent.

FEDERAL, STATE, AND LOCAL NONDEFENSE EXPENDITURES, BY MAJOR PURPOSE, AS PERCENTAGES OF GDP, 1959 AND 1992

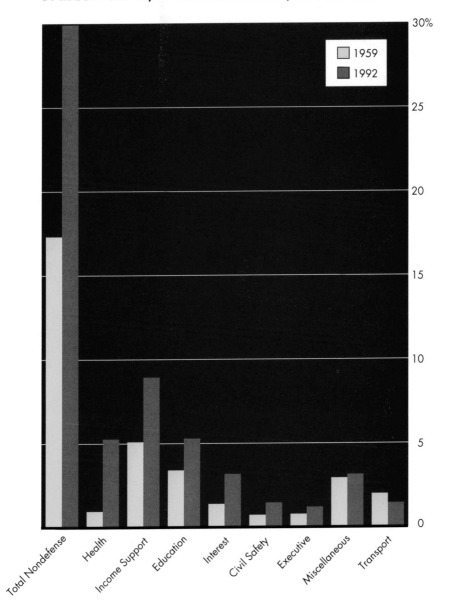

Federal payments directed specifically to low-income persons have been rising but are still only about 2¹/₂ percent of GDP.

By 1993 federal payments to individuals had risen to 56 percent of total federal outlays, from 27 percent in 1962. This category of outlays consists of transfer payments, not in exchange for goods sold or services provided or money lent to the government (interest). Payments to individuals constituted 85 percent of all federal outlays other than for national defense and interest. This allocation of outlays reveals a government whose main function, except for defense, is shifting money around from taxpayers to various beneficiaries, most of whom are also taxpayers.

Between 1962 and 1993, federal payments to individuals rose from 5.2 percent of GDP to 10.5 percent. In 1993 about 57 percent of these payments were for social security and Medicare. Payments under these programs had increased greatly as a result of the growth of the beneficiary population—mainly the aged—and benefit increases due to legislative changes, increases in earnings histories of retiring workers, and higher medical costs. Large additional amounts went for the retirement benefits of federal workers and for veterans.

Federal payments to people eligible for benefits only because they are poor—"means-tested" benefits—rose from under 1 percent of GDP to about 2¹/₂ percent between 1962 and 1993. This amount consisted mainly of payments under the Medicaid, food stamp, and public assistance programs. In 1993 they constituted about 14 percent of total federal outlays.

FEDERAL PAYMENTS TO INDIVIDUALS
AS PERCENTAGES OF GDP, 1962–1993

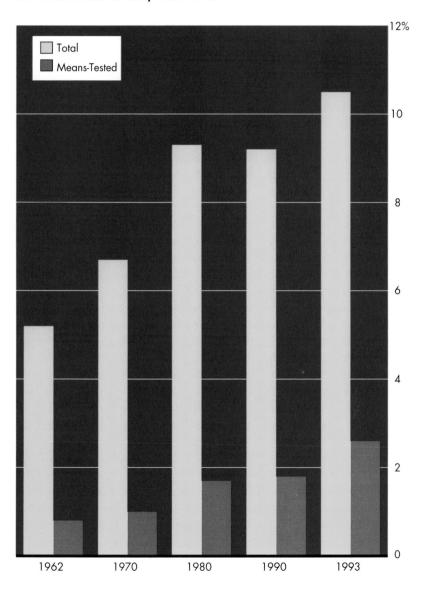

The ratio of the benefits received under social security to the taxes paid for any individual depends on his time of retirement and family status.

A basic principle of the social security system has been that in the aggregate beneficiaries would receive in benefits the value of the taxes paid plus interest accumulated during their working lives. Whether this rationale holds true in the long run, it is not true for individual beneficiaries, whose returns are highly unequal.

When the system was established in 1935, it was clear that the first retirees would have few years of covered employment. To provide them with what seemed adequate retirement benefits, the system was arranged so that the ratio of benefits to covered earnings would be higher for people with low covered earnings than for those with higher covered earnings. Moreover, as time passed, social security taxes and benefit rates were raised, and the higher benefits were made available to people who had formerly paid tax at the lower rates. The combination of these two factors created a situation, illustrated in the chart, in which people who were born earlier and people who earned lower incomes received much more benefit relative to the payments on their account than those who were born later.

The chart shows the number of years of receiving benefits that would be required for a worker to recover the social security taxes that had been paid on his behalf plus interest. (The figures refer to a single worker retiring at age sixty-five and assume a real interest rate of 2.3 percent.) As can be seen, a worker who was born in 1895 and who had the minimum earnings would recover his tax payments in less than a year. But a worker with the average earnings born in 1965 will require nineteen years of benefits to recover his payments; and if he had the maximum covered earnings, thirty-three years would be required.

Family status also makes a big difference in the amount of benefits retired workers receive relative to their payments. In general, the returns are greatest for married couples with a single earner, mainly because of the payment of benefits to spouses and survivors who did not work in addition to the normal benefits paid to the working spouse. The advantage to the married couple is increased by the greater life expectancy of the survivor in a two-person family than of either a single male or a single female.

YEARS OF RETIREMENT NEEDED TO RECOVER SOCIAL SECURITY TAXES, 1895, 1935, AND 1965

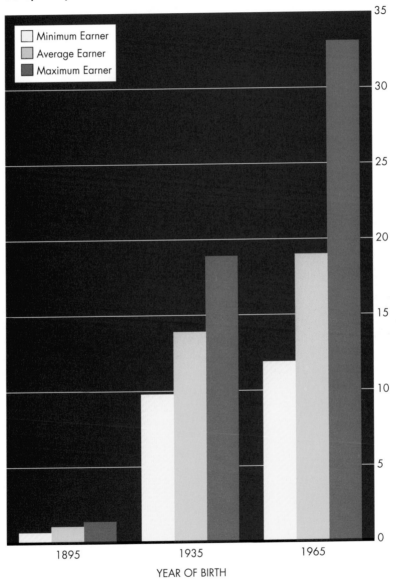

Since the early 1950s, federal employment has declined substantially as a fraction of total employment.

Although the path of federal employment shows bulges during the Korean War and the Vietnam War, its declining trend relative to total employment is clear. This decline occurred despite a large rise in real federal expenditures relative to GDP during this period.

Between 1950 and 1994, the number of federal employees increased by about 40 percent, whereas real federal expenditures increased by about 340 percent. The rise in federal expenditures was concentrated in programs that used relatively few people to pay out large amounts of money. Expenditures for social security, Medicare, and interest are leading examples. Real federal expenditures per federal employee more than tripled between 1950 and 1994.

Almost one-third of all federal civilian employees work for the Department of Defense. The next largest agency is the Treasury, which has about 5 percent of all federal civilian employees.

FEDERAL EMPLOYMENT
AS PERCENTAGE OF TOTAL EMPLOYMENT, 1950–1994

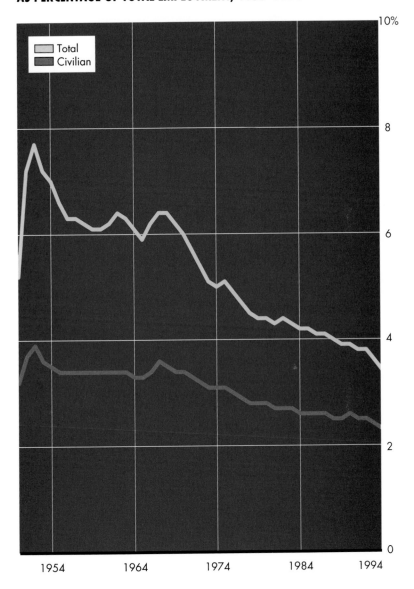

Total federal revenues, as a percentage of GDP, have been on a slightly rising trend since the end of World War II as the increase of payroll taxes has offset the decline of all other taxes combined.

At their peak in World War II, federal taxes were about 22 percent of GDP. Tax cuts after the war brought the ratio down to about 15 percent, but soon thereafter the ratio moved up into the range of 18 to 20 percent. Since 1960 the ratio has been below 18 percent in only four years and as high as 20 percent in only two years. In 1994 it was 19 percent.

The ratio rose to 20 percent in fiscal 1969, when a temporary surtax was imposed to help finance the Vietnam War. It then declined when the surtax expired. The ratio began to rise again after 1978 as inflation pushed income-tax payers into higher brackets. The 1981 tax cut undid that increase.

Although the ratio of total revenue to GDP has fluctuated within a narrow range, the composition of the revenue has changed substantially. The big change was the rise in the payroll tax. Receipts from all other sources declined as a percentage of GDP, largely due to a decline in corporate taxes. Corporate profits fell relative to GDP, and the effective rate of taxation on corporate profits also fell. Individual income tax receipts as a percentage of GDP showed no clear trend after 1952. Although income tax rates were reduced from time to time, these reductions served mainly to offset the rise of income tax burdens that resulted from the interaction of economic growth and inflation with a progressive tax structure. Since 1981, indexation of the individual income tax has eliminated the increase of the individual tax burden that results from inflation.

Receipts from payroll taxes increased from 1.7 percent of GDP in 1950 to 7.0 percent in 1994. Social security payroll tax rates were raised, the ceiling on wages subject to the tax was increased, coverage was expanded, and a new tax was imposed for Medicare beginning in 1966.

The payroll tax revenues are dedicated to specific purposes—retirement and disability insurance, medical insurance, and unemployment insurance. The revenues available for financing all other functions of government have been on a declining trend, relative to GDP, since 1950. In 1994 they were lower than in any year before 1983 back to the 1930s.

FEDERAL REVENUES AS PERCENTAGE OF GDP, 1948–1994

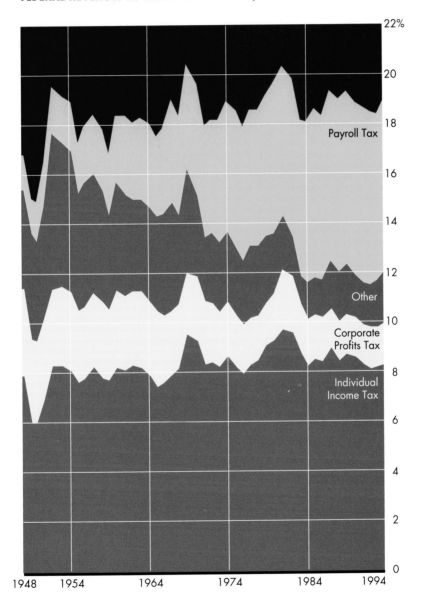

Except for the introduction of the earned-income credit, federal income taxes in 1994 were about the same as in 1970 for families at a wide range of income levels.

In 1994 a married couple with two dependents and an income of $35,000 in 1990 dollars (about $39,500 in 1994 dollars) would have paid 8.9 percent of its income in federal income tax. In 1970 a similar family with a similar real income would have paid 11.7 percent. For a couple with an income of $75,000 in 1990 dollars, there was almost no change in the percentage of income paid in tax between 1970 and 1994. For the $35,000 family, the marginal tax rate—the percentage of an additional dollar of income that would be paid as tax—declined somewhat, from 19.5 percent to 15 percent, and for the $75,000 family it was essentially unchanged.

The taxation of the lowest-income families changed dramatically, however. In 1970 a family with $10,000 of income in 1990 dollars would have paid no income tax. In 1994, under the earned-income credit, it would have received a refund equal to 22 percent of its income. But in 1994 it was subject to a marginal rate of 17.7 percent. That is, its earned-income credit would have declined by 17.7 percent of any additional income it earned.

(These calculations relate to families that have one earner, all of whose income is taxable, and take the standard deductions. The results would differ somewhat for families in different circumstances.)

AVERAGE FEDERAL INCOME TAX RATE AS PERCENTAGE OF INCOME, 1970, 1988, AND 1994

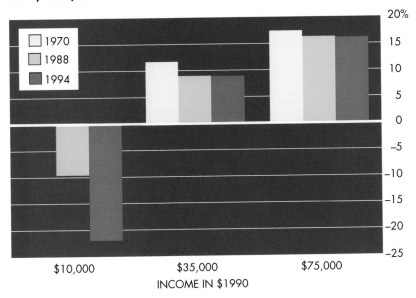

NOTE: Average tax rate for $10,000 class was zero in 1970.

MARGINAL FEDERAL INCOME TAX RATE AS PERCENTAGE OF ADDITIONAL INCOME, 1970, 1988, AND 1994

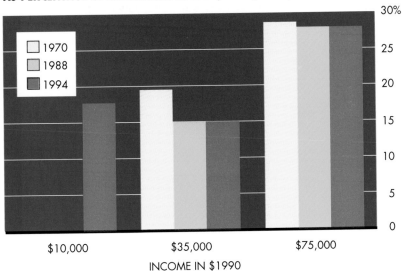

NOTE: Marginal tax rate for $10,000 class was zero in 1970 and 1988.

Total government receipts and expenditures as a percentage of GDP are low in the United States compared with other industrial countries.

In 1993 both government expenditures and government receipts were lower relative to GDP than in the average of European industrial countries. In fact, in none of the European countries was the receipts-to-GDP ratio lower than in the United States, and only in Switzerland was the expenditures-to-GDP ratio lower than in the United States—and that by a small amount. In Japan, expenditures are minutely lower, relative to GDP, than in the United States, but receipts are a little higher.

The ratios of both expenditures and receipts to GDP have risen in all countries over the past twenty years and probably much longer. The rise in the United States, though, has been smaller than in other countries.

During the period covered here, the United States has spent more of its GDP on defense than other countries. The higher ratio of spending to GDP in Europe is due to higher expenditures there for social welfare programs.

GOVERNMENT RECEIPTS
AS PERCENTAGE OF GDP, 1968, 1978, AND 1993

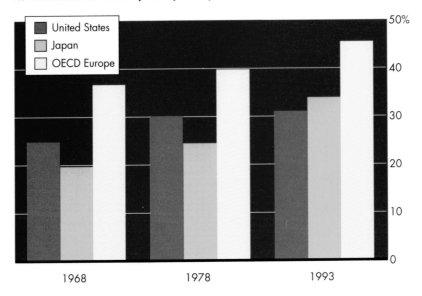

GOVERNMENT EXPENDITURES
AS PERCENTAGE OF GDP, 1968, 1978, AND 1993

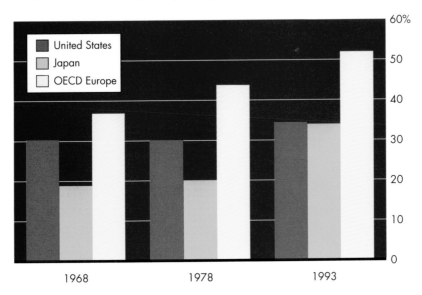

Except for wars and recessions, until recently total federal receipts and expenditures have moved closely together.

World War II (1941–1945), the Korean War (1950–1953), and the Vietnam War (1965–1973) stand out in the chart, as do the depression of the 1930s and the recessions of 1958 and 1975. The deficits of the 1980s were also affected by the defense buildup and the recession of 1981–1982. The continuation of a significant deficit into the late 1980s and early 1990s, even in fairly prosperous years and despite a substantial decline in defense expenditures relative to GDP, was an exception to the earlier pattern. An important reason was that the rise of expenditures for health, social security, and interest had offset about half the decline in defense expenditures. Nonetheless, in 1994 the deficit, as a percentage of GDP, was smaller than in any year since 1981. With the programs in effect at the end of 1994, that ratio is likely to continue to decline through the end of the century but begin to rise soon thereafter.

FEDERAL EXPENDITURES, RECEIPTS, AND DEFICIT AS PERCENTAGES OF GDP, 1929–1994

FISCAL YEAR

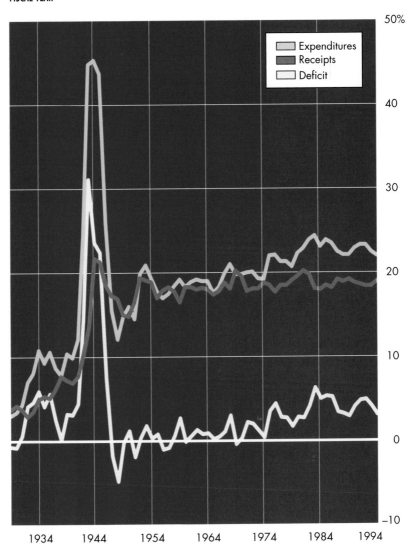

The federal debt and the interest on it have both risen substantially in relation to the GDP since the early 1970s.

The federal debt rose enormously during World War II and reached a level in excess of the GDP of the time. But although the debt continued to increase as a result of budget deficits, the ratio of the debt to the GDP fell sharply. Between the end of 1946 and the end of 1974, the absolute size of the debt rose by more than 40 percent, but as a percentage of GDP it fell from 114 percent to 24 percent. That decline was, of course, due to the strong rise of GDP, partly resulting from inflation. In fact, during that period the real value of the debt—that is, the debt adjusted for the increase in the consumer price index—fell by almost 45 percent.

After 1974 the ratio of the debt to the GDP began to rise, as the size of deficits increased relative to the growth of the GDP. In the early 1990s, there were signs that the ratio was stabilizing, at least temporarily, in the neighborhood of 50 percent. Even though deficits persisted, their size relative to the growth of GDP was not high enough to cause the ratio of debt to GDP to rise.

The interest burden—the ratio of federal interest to GDP—fell after World War II, but fell less rapidly than the debt-to-GDP ratio and rose after 1974, but more rapidly than the debt-to-GDP ratio. This increase reflected the rise of the interest rate on the outstanding debt, as market interest rates rose and as the World War II debt, which had been incurred at extremely low rates, had to be refinanced at higher rates. But since 1984, the interest burden has also stabilized between 3.0 and 3.5 percent of GDP, partly because interest rates have subsided from the extraordinary peak reached around 1980.

The figures shown here refer to the debt held by the public and the interest on that debt. That is, it excludes debt held by federal government accounts, mainly the Social Security Trust Fund. The general pattern shown in the charts would also be true of the total debt, except that its level would be higher and its increase over the entire period would be greater.

FEDERAL DEBT HELD BY PUBLIC AS PERCENTAGE OF GDP, 1940–1994

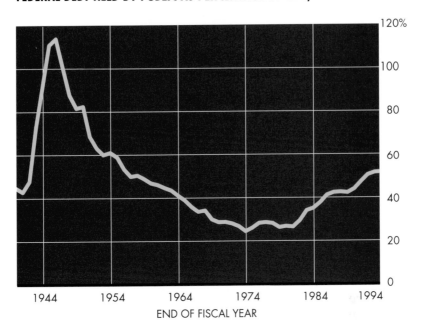

END OF FISCAL YEAR

FEDERAL NET INTEREST AS PERCENTAGE OF GDP, 1940–1994

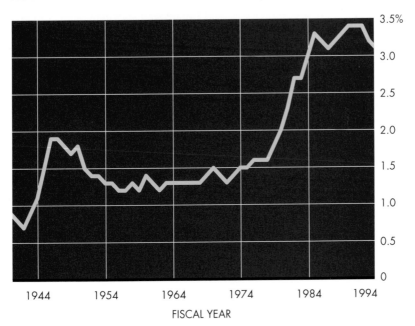

FISCAL YEAR

Fluctuations of the economy cause major fluctuations in the federal deficit or surplus.

A rise of the economy, with increasing incomes, raises the tax base and raises the revenue if tax rates are unchanged. Expenditures for unemployment compensation also fall as the economy rises, and some other expenditures tied to earnings or employment also decline. Thus the deficit declines or the surplus rises as the economy rises.

The chart shows the actual surplus, as a percentage of GDP, and an estimate of what the surplus would have been each year, as a percentage of GDP, if the economy had been at high employment in each year.

This response of the budget to cyclical changes in the economy is commonly considered to be an "automatic stabilizer" of the economy, tending to limit the size of economic fluctuations. When the economy declines and income falls, private after-tax incomes fall less than they would otherwise, because some of the decline of incomes is absorbed in a decline of taxes. In addition, part of the loss of private incomes is made up by unemployment compensation and other government payments. This cushioning of the decline in private after-tax incomes tends to limit the decline in private spending and so to limit the multiplication of the forces of decline in the economy.

This stabilizing effect is called "automatic" because it occurs without any decision by government to change tax or expenditure programs. The response does not depend on the accuracy of government forecasts. Moreover, the response does not involve any change of government programs that might be inconsistent with longer-run objectives.

While the power of this automatic stabilizing effect is uncertain, there is no doubt about the desirability of distinguishing between the behavior of the budget deficit or surplus due to cyclical, temporary fluctuations of the economy and that due to more durable conditions and policies.

The chart shows large fluctuations in the size of the deficit relative to GDP, even aside from the fluctuations brought on by cyclical changes in the economy. The outstanding cases were the big rises in the high-employment deficit during the Vietnam War and during the defense buildup of the early 1980s and the subsequent reduction as defense expenditures declined relative to GDP.

HIGH-EMPLOYMENT DEFICITS AND ACTUAL DEFICITS AS PERCENTAGE OF POTENTIAL GDP, 1962–1994

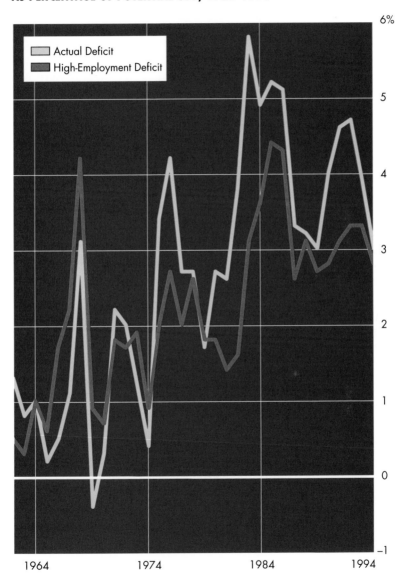

Different plausible definitions yield very different calculations of the size of the federal deficit.

There are two main reasons for measuring the federal deficit. One, a "disciplinary" reason, is to see how far, if at all, the government is giving benefits to people, through expenditures, without assessing the costs, through taxes. The other is to see how far, if at all, the government is depressing investment by absorbing saving that would otherwise be invested.

Although measurements of the deficit are useful for these purposes, no single measure or combination of measures is completely satisfactory. The government can provide benefits that do not appear in any measure of expenditures, for example, by mandating states, localities, and private parties to provide benefits to others, or by guaranteeing loans, or by issuing regulations. The government also affects investment by its own investment expenditures, by promising future benefits that influence private saving, and by the character of its taxes.

To illustrate the absence of any unique all-purpose measure of the deficit, the chart shows estimates of the deficit for fiscal 1994 on five different plausible definitions:

A.   the conventional "cash-consolidated" deficit

B.   the same deficit but excluding the trust accounts, mainly social security, on the ground that the assets of these accounts belong not to the government but to designated beneficiaries and are balanced, or more than balanced, by liabilities to them

C.   the change in a comprehensive measure of the net liabilities of the federal government including the Federal Reserve system, taking account of the value of capital assets such as infrastructure and gold, all adjusted for inflation

D.   the deficit in the National Income and Product Accounts, which differs from A mainly in not including loan transactions. This deficit fits into the equation that the deficit plus private investment equals private saving plus the capital inflow

E.   the excess of the deficit of type A over the amount that would keep the ratio of federal debt to GDP constant

THE FEDERAL BUDGET DEFICIT
ACCORDING TO VARIOUS DEFINITIONS, FISCAL 1994

BILLIONS OF $

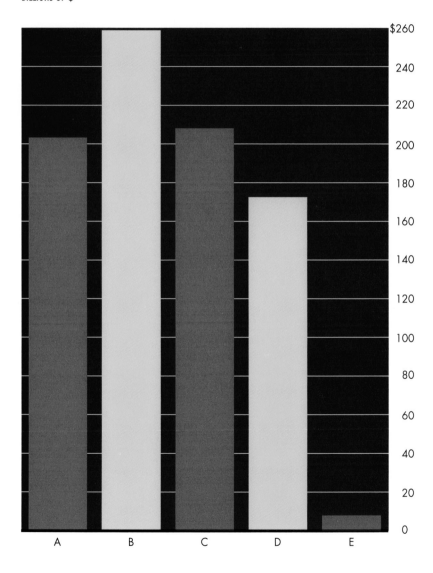

PART FOURTEEN

Health

National health
expenditures were close to
$900 billion in 1993, or
almost 14 percent of GDP.
According to the Health Care
Financing Administration (HCFA),
more than 88.5 percent of national health expenditures went for personal
health care in 1993. The remainder represented the net cost of private
health insurance (premiums less benefits) and of the administrative
expense of government programs like Medicare and Medicaid (5.4 percent); government public health activities (2.8 percent); and research and
hospital construction (3.3 percent). By personal care is meant spending for
hospital services, services of doctors and dentists, drugs and medicines,
nursing homes, and home health care. These categories are arbitrary in that
persons are the ultimate beneficiaries of all health expenditures—private
insurance, research, hospital construction, and public health programs.

Private insurance costs in 1993 were $38 billion. This represents the
difference between insurance premiums of $296 billion and benefits of
$258 billion, which in turn represent 33.5 percent and 29.2 percent of
national health expenditures. Private insurance embraces not only conventional health insurance but also Blue Cross–Blue Shield, health main-
tenance organizations, and arrangements like preferred provider
organizations, which have become prominent in recent years.

In 1965, when Medicare and Medicaid were enacted, national health
expenditures were 5.9 percent and personal care 5.1 percent of GDP (top
chart). Their increased share of GDP since then can be attributed not only
to the new government programs but also to the rise of incomes generally
and the spread of private health insurance. In 1965 the net cost of private
insurance and the administrative cost of running government programs
were somewhat lower (4.6 percent), public health much lower (1.5 percent), and research and hospital construction combined much higher (8.2
percent).

The pie charts show breakdowns of personal consumption expenditures in 1965 and 1993. In 1993 the biggest share of the consumer health
dollar went to hospitals, followed by physicians' services and other pro-
fessional services, like dentists, chiropractors, and podiatrists. Changes
in percentage shares from 1965 to 1993, which reflect changes in both
prices and physical volume, are striking in the case of drugs and medicines, whose share fell drastically, and of nursing homes, whose share
rose considerably. The hospital share was also higher, but there was little
change in the share taken by doctors and other professionals.

DISTRIBUTION OF PERSONAL HEALTH EXPENDITURES, BY TYPE, 1993

PERCENT

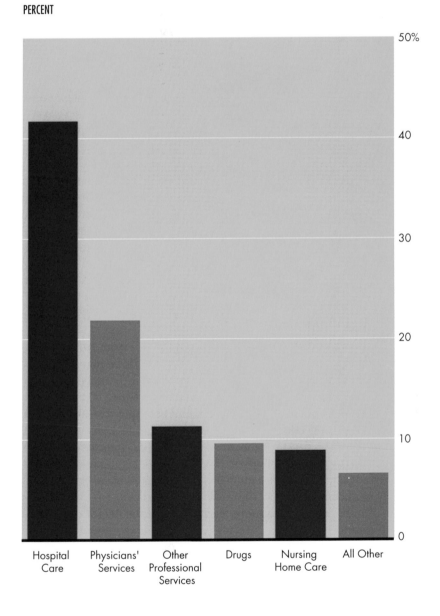

From 1977 to 1992, the
health services industry
experienced roughly
average growth in output
and much greater than
average growth in prices
and employment.

When consumers make expenditures for medical care, they purchase what the health care industry produces—the services of private doctors, nurses, medical labs, and hospitals—and what other industries produce as well: that is, drugs and medicines, food eaten in hospitals and nursing homes, eyeglasses, and wheelchairs. What is referred to as the *health services industry* leaves out all government-run hospitals plus all health personnel on government payrolls. The private sector, including the nonprofit part, is by far the larger sector in this country.

Since the early postwar period the health services industry has grown about 50 percent faster than the private economy. That growth, however, has not been steady. Physical volume, which had grown at an annual rate of 5.6 percent from 1947 to 1977, grew at a rate of only 2.4 percent from 1977 to 1992. In the latest fifteen-year period, domestic output of all private industries grew a bit faster—at a 2.6 percent rate.

The price of output of health services—increasing about 5 percent a year from 1947 to 1977—rose more than 8 percent per year from 1977 to 1992. Prices for all domestic private industries grew at a 5 percent rate over the latest fifteen-year period.

Even though its output grew at an average rate from 1977 to 1992, employment in the health care industry increased at three times the average private industry rate from 1977 to 1992. This growth implies a deterioration in productivity and suggests rising labor costs per unit of output. Indeed, employee-compensation costs per unit of output rose about twice as fast as for all domestic private industry from 1977 to 1992.

Health output has probably grown faster than indicated because price changes are not being measured properly. Quality improvements as a result of advances in medical knowledge and technological change have probably not been adequately captured by the price indexes, which thus have an upward bias. Furthermore, the services of the doctor or the hospital are intermediate inputs. We really want to know about final outcomes—the health and well-being of the people. Even with these qualifications there can be no denying that labor costs and prices in the health field have been rising very rapidly.

ANNUAL RATE OF CHANGE IN OUTPUT, PRICES, AND EMPLOYMENT IN THE HEALTH SERVICES INDUSTRY AND ALL PRIVATE INDUSTRY, 1977–1992

PERCENT

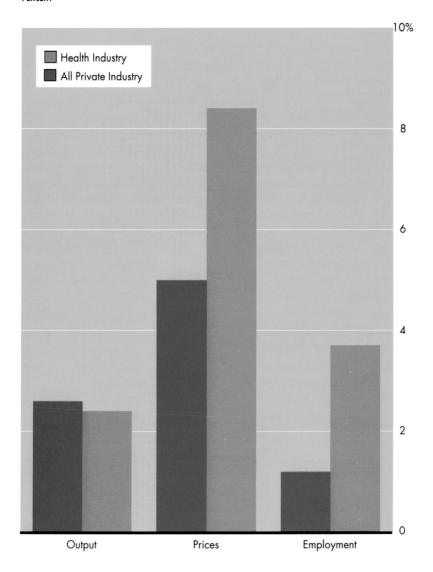

In the past thirty years,
out-of-pocket
expenditures on health
care have declined, while
third-party payments
have increased.

In 1965, when Medicare and Medicaid were enacted, individuals made out-of-pocket payments for 55 percent of their health care expenditures. Private health insurance accounted for about one-fourth of the total and government for about one-fifth. At that time government meant mainly the Veterans' Administration hospitals of the federal government and state and local hospitals and clinics.

Since then, as the chart shows, striking changes have occurred. Probably the most important economically is the sharp decline in the importance of out-of-pocket payments, which fell to 20 percent of the total in 1993, and the complementary rise in third-party payments. Medicare and Medicaid combined now finance one-third of total expenditures, and private insurance accounts for another one-third. The old government programs now account for only 10 percent, but government as a whole finances 43 percent of total expenditures, not counting taxes foregone.

Analysts point to the decline in out-of-pocket payments as the single most important reason for the rapid escalation in health care costs in the past three decades and for the distortions brought on by a partially regulated health care system. Taxpayers at all levels of government pay for Medicaid, whose benefits go to low-income persons. It is said that Medicaid payments to hospitals and doctors reimburse much less than the costs incurred. To a lesser extent this is also true of Medicare, which covers older and disabled people regardless of income and is paid for by payroll taxes on employers and employees, by premiums, and by general revenues. These Medicare and Medicaid services are provided by the health care industry, making up for inadequate government payments by shifting costs to all other patients and especially to persons completely lacking in any kind of health insurance.

What is not known about the U.S. health care system, with its high costs and many distortions, is how the health of the population has been affected. We do not know whether the same health services could have been obtained at lower cost or whether the high costs that seem so common have in fact brought about better results that are not now obvious on some comprehensive basis.

PERCENTAGE DISTRIBUTION OF PERSONAL HEALTH EXPENDITURES BY SOURCE OF FINANCING, 1960–1993

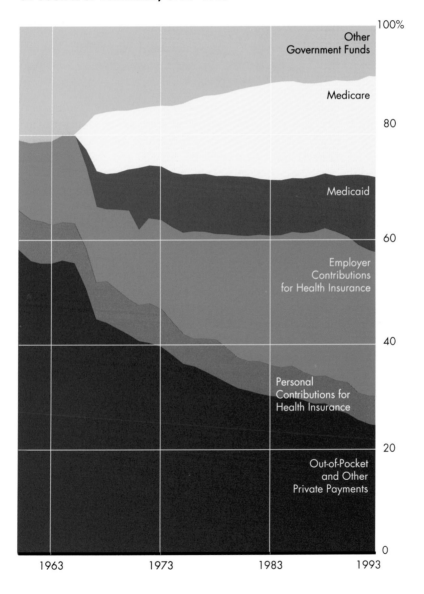

Other Government Funds

Medicare

Medicaid

Employer Contributions for Health Insurance

Personal Contributions for Health Insurance

Out-of-Pocket and Other Private Payments

100%

80

60

40

20

0

1963   1973   1983   1993

Most persons who have
health insurance provided
by employers enjoy a
large subsidy.
A large part of the population covered by health insurance is being
subsidized by government. The benefits come at the expense of those not
covered by insurance or those who buy their own. Employees have
always had the option of taking part of their compensation in the form of
nontaxable fringe benefits rather than taxable wages or salaries. With
some exceptions, people who buy their own insurance cannot deduct any
medical expenses from taxable income. In addition, self-employed persons have been able to deduct part of their insurance premiums since
1987. The CBO has estimated that the exclusion of employer-provided
health insurance meant a loss of $73 billion in income and payroll taxes
in 1994. Using a different approach, the Joint Committee on Taxation
estimated the tax loss in 1995 at $90 billion.

In 1992, about three out of four workers were covered by insurance
provided by their own employers or the employers of other family members. The higher the wage, the higher the coverage: in 1992, 40 percent for
those earning $5 an hour or less, but 93 percent for those earning $15 an
hour or more.

The CBO has estimated the average tax subsidy of employment-
based health insurance to families by size of family income. The average
subsidy was estimated to be $1,130, which was 26 percent of the average
premium. This proportion rose from 11 percent for families with income
below $10,000 to 33 percent for families with incomes of $200,000 or
more. The charts illustrate three other points:

• As a percentage of after-tax income for families with employ-
ment-based health insurance, the subsidy varied from 2 to 3.5 percent
over a broad range of incomes.

• As a percentage of after-tax income for all families—those
with and those without employer-based insurance—the percentage rises
as income rises, reaching about 2.3 percent at $20,000 and staying at
about that level, except for families with incomes above $100,000.

• The after-tax premium is 7 percent of after-tax income for all
families. It is 9–10 percent for families with after-tax income between
$20,000 and $50,000.

TAX SUBSIDY AS PERCENTAGE OF AFTER-TAX INCOME, BY INCOME CLASS, 1992

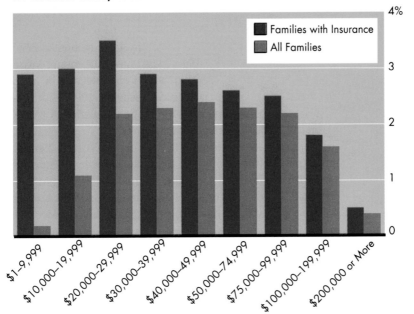

PREMIUM AS PERCENTAGE OF INCOME, BY INCOME CLASS, 1992

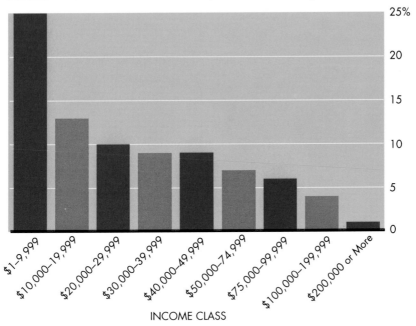

INCOME CLASS

Lack of any kind of health insurance was one of the main reasons that health care became a major political issue in 1993 and 1994. The chart shows insurance coverage for the U.S. population for 1980, 1987, and 1993, on the basis of Census Bureau surveys.

Although employer expenditures in the form of fringe benefits increased over the period, the number of individuals covered decreased considerably, as costs of insurance escalated rapidly. Persons with no insurance went from 11 to 15 percent of the population. This statistic includes working people with incomes too high to qualify for Medicaid but too low to buy insurance, plus those persons (especially young people) who could buy insurance but prefer not to because they consider the risk of costly illness to be too low. Coverage data show a direct relationship between income level or wage level and the existence of insurance. From 1980 to 1983, the Medicare group went from 11 to 13 percent of the population, and the Medicaid group from 5 to 8 percent.

Lapses in insurance were also a prominent issue in the health care debate. The Census Bureau found that in the twelve months of 1990, 80 percent of the population had continuous health insurance coverage. When the time period was extended to thirty months (February 1990–September 1992), however, continuous coverage dropped to 75 percent. Lapses varied inversely with age, amount of education, and income level.

PERCENTAGE DISTRIBUTION OF THE POPULATION
BY PRIMARY SOURCE OF HEALTH INSURANCE, 1980, 1987, AND 1993

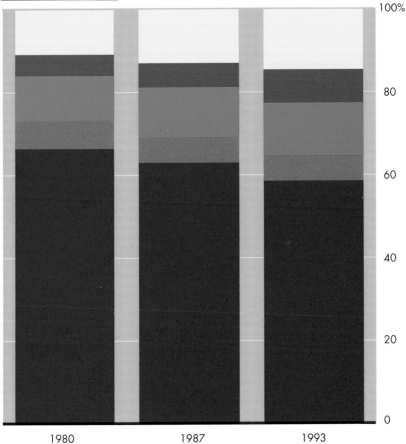

PART FIFTEEN

Quality of Life

Conventional measures of economic progress—per capita real GDP or consumption—leave much to be desired despite their usefulness.

Some measurement problems that affect the GDP remain inherently difficult, and of these, the most important is the measurement of price change. For all the considerable care the price indexes receive, they have their problems, among them:

- *The treatment of quality change.* At the heart of the BLS approach to price measurement is "specification pricing." To get a price change from month 1 to month 2, BLS wants to make sure that the item being priced in month 2 is the same quality as the item priced in month 1. So for each item it establishes specifications that describe the item's characteristics as well as the kind of store selling the item. But suppliers come out with new models frequently and make improvements for which they may charge different prices or permit quality to vary while price remains unchanged. Keeping track of these price-mixed-with-quality changes is not easy.

- *Innovations.* The treatment of innovations is perhaps the most difficult aspect of handling quality change. Computers are a prime example. Knowing what to do with computer prices had baffled both the Bureau of Labor Statistics and the Commerce Department. For many years the Commerce Department clung to an admittedly poor assumption that computer prices were unchanged. Finally in 1985 it introduced a new price index for computers. The chart shows the new implicit prices for computers bought by business now embodied in the estimates of real GDP.

- *Pricing inputs instead of outputs.* Closely related to the treatment of innovations is the practice of pricing inputs instead of outcomes or outputs. BLS does not measure the cost of lighting as such, for example, but it does measure the price of electricity. But this practice ignores the fact that more energy-efficient bulbs and lamps have appeared on the market.

- *Outlet shifts.* Traditionally, BLS has treated a given item sold in a big chain store as different from the same item sold in a small independent, because the two types of store are presumed to offer different services: thus the fact that the price in the chain store is lower than that in the independent is missed in the BLS treatment. So is much of the increased market share won by the chains, with its price-lowering effect.

IMPLICIT PRICE DEFLATORS FOR COMPUTERS, 1960-1994

INDEX: 1987=100, LOGARITHMIC SCALE

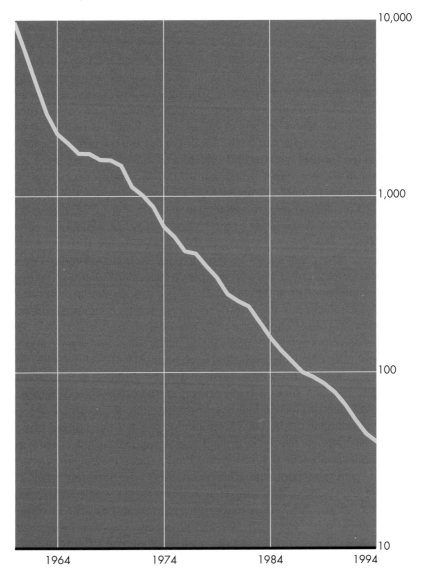

GDP is not a measure of welfare.

Our well-being and how much our lives have improved over the years depend on much more than flows of goods and services that pass through markets. Hours spent off the job in housework and raising children are also important. Our well-being depends on how much leisure we have, on the social and political conditions under which we do our paid and unpaid work and spend our leisure hours, on our health as well as on our physical environment, and on the public capital and the private capital we have in the form of housing and consumer durables. The last point is illustrated in the top chart, which shows the ownership of various consumer durables in 1993. All households have refrigerators, practically all have gas or electric ranges, and 98 percent own color TVs. Twenty-three percent of all households in the United States had a personal computer in 1993.

These aspects of how we live are so common today that they are taken for granted, but that was not so early in the twentieth century. Some examples of how things have changed are shown in the bottom chart, which illustrates the prevalence of electricity, complete plumbing facilities, and telephones since 1900. Even as recently as 1940, only 55 percent of households had complete plumbing facilities, and a generation ago one out of five households lacked a telephone.

While these figures point to genuine progress, a fundamental problem remains: there is really no way statistics alone can capture the convenience of electric lighting, of private indoor toilet facilities, and of a telephone in the house. This limitation remains even though the personal consumption figures in the NIPA make allowance for a rising quality of housing services that Americans have experienced over the years.

A generation ago, when economists began to show greater interest in how to measure changes in well-being—for worse as well as for better—it was fashionable to discuss traffic congestion, the increase in commuting time, and environmental problems. Today social problems have come to the fore. We have statistics on crime and illegitimacy, but it is not enough to point to the rise in crime and illegitimate births. The problem, which is probably unsolvable, is to put all these statistics together in a unified framework embracing what is already included in measured real per capita income or consumption.

PERCENTAGE OF HOUSEHOLDS OWNING VARIOUS DURABLE GOODS, 1993

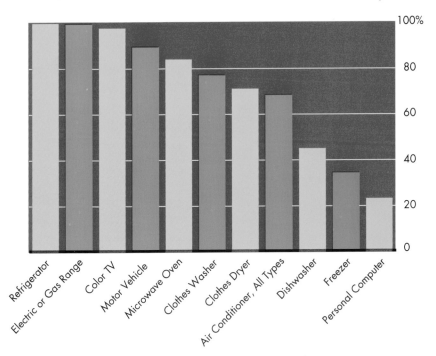

PERCENTAGE OF U.S. HOMES WITH VARIOUS AMENITIES, 1900–1990

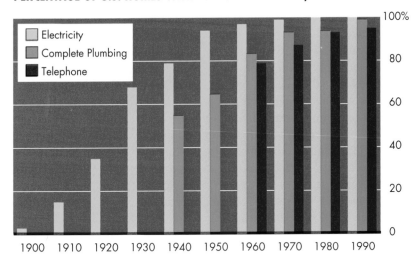

NOTE: Statistics for complete plumbing and telephones were not available until 1940 and 1960, respectively.

Environmental issues
highlight the difficulties
economists have in
assessing how welfare has
been affected.

Since 1972, real expenditures by consumers, business, and government for pollution abatement and control have almost doubled. Business expenditures were 64 percent of the 1992 total.

Expenditures for pollution control increase costs and become part of measured GDP, but whether they should be included is a matter of debate. They are made to restore the natural environment to a previously superior condition and to prevent future pollution. Their inclusion exaggerates the growth of productivity and real income. According to the late Edward Denison, however, any correction for the overstatement in productivity growth should be limited to those expenditures made by business, not by what consumers and governments spend. Focusing on *measured* GDP, Denison argued that if consumers did not make expenditures for emission abatement devices on their automobiles, they would probably make expenditures of comparable size on other things. The same is true of such expenditures by governments. New pollution regulations imposed on business, however, require business to incur costs they would not otherwise have incurred. The regulations give us a cleaner and healthier environment than would be found in their absence, but the resources used could ultimately have been devoted to other consumption.

Business costs for pollution abatement and control were about 1 percent of GDP in 1992, about double the 1972 percentage. The productivity data used in this book do not make allowance for business pollution expenditures. If they did, the doubling of the ratio from 1972 to 1992 would have the effect of reducing productivity growth slightly.

Although cleaner air and water are genuine benefits, they are not now part of measured GDP, nor are the health benefits that come from a cleaner environment. The determination and valuation of these benefits pose formidable problems. Thus, although many common air pollutants have decreased since 1970 in the face of rising economic activity and automobile use (see chart), our current national accounts do not show the benefits. The satellite accounts discussed elsewhere would represent a step in the right direction.

POLLUTION ABATEMENT EXPENDITURES BY SECTOR, 1972–1992

BILLIONS OF $1987

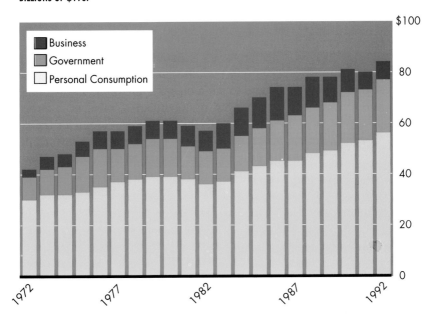

NATIONAL AIR POLLUTANT EMISSIONS, BY POLLUTANT, 1940–1992

1970 QUANTITIES=100

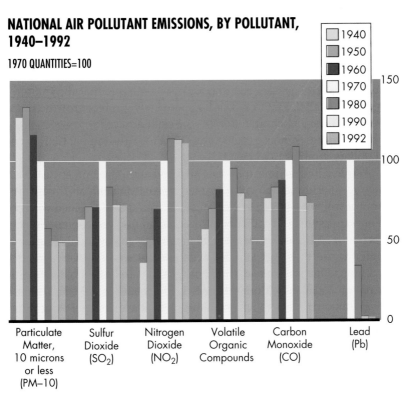

Attempts to construct indexes of economic welfare have not gained widespread acceptance. Economists have attempted to go beyond the market-based national income and product accounts to get a closer approximation of welfare. This attempt involves "pushing out the boundaries" of what is already measured. The most common extensions make imputations for the services of consumer and government capital, the value of housework performed by the housewife, and, in some instances, the value of leisure "consumed" by individuals. Some of these are easier to estimate than others. For example, we have discussed how the value of services of consumer capital might be estimated, as well as the difficulties in evaluating government services. This is a general problem when there is no market. Should housework, for example, be valued at what economists call opportunity cost, which might or might not be the hourly wage an individual earns on the job? Comparisons over a period of years require inflation adjustments, but whether the deflator should be the wage rate or the CPI is not clear.

These efforts have been undertaken by a number of economists. Because such estimates cover a broader range of activities, those totals have been greater than the official GNP or GDP totals. Summarizing these investigations, Robert Eisner in 1989 noted that the alternative measures show somewhat less growth from the early postwar years to the early 1980s, but differences are not major. It is interesting that these alternatives, like the official figures, exhibit a slowdown in real growth starting in the mid-1970s. The chart illustrates the estimates of Professor Eisner in his Total Incomes System of Accounts (TISA) and the official GNP, in constant dollars, from 1946 to 1981.

Another line of research has involved the development of social indicators—pertaining to health, crime, the environment, and many other aspects of welfare—which in some fashion would be combined with conventional measures of real income or consumption per capita. This task is much more difficult because social indicators go beyond the market to a greater degree than the extended accounts discussed above. Aside from this, if individual preferences vary, how are they to be combined? Earlier research on social indicators was criticized because it lacked a good theoretical framework. Although social problems have become more important than before, we are still a long way from having a measure that would be widely accepted.

THE OFFICIAL GNP MEASURE AND THE TOTAL INCOMES SYSTEM OF ACCOUNTS MEASURE OF REAL OUTPUT, 1946–1981

BILLIONS OF CONSTANT $, LOGARITHMIC SCALE

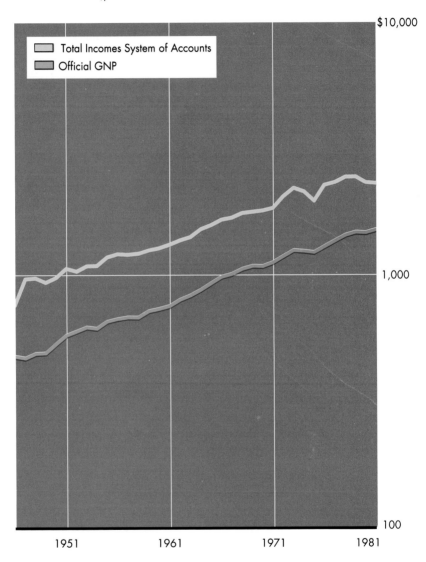

PART SIXTEEN

The United States in the World Economy

Since the 1960s, U.S. international economic transactions have increased greatly as a percentage of GDP.

The chart shows total payments on current account—that is, it excludes capital transactions such as investment flows in or out of the country. The payments included are for the purchase of goods and services, investment income, and unilateral transfers, such as private remittances and foreign aid. The largest item on both sides is the export or import of merchandise, although the international flow of services has become increasingly important.

The increase in foreign transactions relative to the GDP resulted in part from reductions of tariffs and other governmental barriers to international trade and from reductions in the costs of transportation and communication. With lower obstacles to trade in goods and services, countries could concentrate on producing the things at which they are relatively efficient and they and their customers gain the benefits of specialization and large-scale production. The increase in international economic transactions has also resulted from large increases in real incomes, especially among the industrial countries but also, more and more, among the newly emerging economies. As incomes have risen, people have become more willing and able to pay for variety in their consumption, including travel. And they have often found variety in foreign products and places.

The greater access of Americans to foreign goods and services, and their increased purchases of them, have improved their standard of living—partly because of the foreign products consumed directly and partly because of the importation of capital goods that has increased productivity. At the same time, the enlarged foreign markets have enabled American businesses and their employees to concentrate on the kinds of production they do best and so to increase their real incomes. Some American businesses and their employees have suffered from the increase of foreign competition, just as some businesses and workers suffer as a result of increased competition from other American businesses and workers. But there is no doubt that the increase in foreign transactions has been a substantial net benefit to Americans.

U.S. FOREIGN PAYMENTS AND RECEIPTS AS PERCENTAGE OF GDP, 1929–1994

EXCLUDING CAPITAL FLOWS

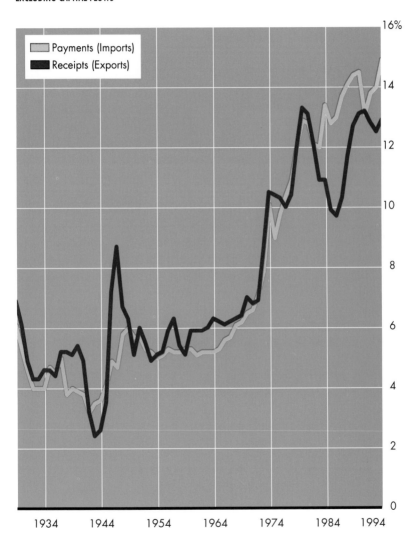

Legend:
- Payments (Imports)
- Receipts (Exports)

Since the early 1980s, U.S. payments abroad, excluding capital transactions, have exceeded U.S. receipts from the rest of the world—a highly unusual situation for the United States in the twentieth century.

In the early days of American history, when the rest of the world was investing heavily in the development of the American economy, U.S. payments to the rest of the world—primarily for imports of goods—typically exceeded U.S. receipts from the rest of the world—primarily for the export of goods. But since 1870 that has been rare. As the chart shows, there was a brief exception during World War II, when U.S. receipts from the rest of the world fell sharply below payments. That happened because most U.S. exports were not sold but were provided by the U.S. government to the Allies under Lend-Lease or otherwise. Thus the excess of payments that began in the 1980s, and especially the magnitude it reached from 1985 to 1987, came as a surprise.

The large increase in U.S. expenditures for imports of petroleum products after 1973, when the oil price had its first sharp rise, was an element in the shift from an excess of receipts to an excess of payments. But even if the cost of the import of petroleum products is excluded, the United States has had an excess of payments since 1983, except for the year 1991. In 1994 the excess of payments was almost 16 percent of total receipts, and 10 percent of receipts if the costs of oil imports are excluded.

U.S. SURPLUS OF FOREIGN RECEIPTS
AS PERCENTAGE OF TOTAL FOREIGN RECEIPTS, 1929–1994

EXCLUDING CAPITAL FLOWS

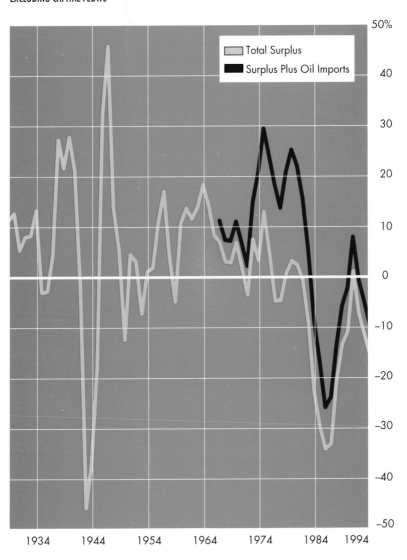

Total Surplus
Surplus Plus Oil Imports

Since 1975, both U.S. exports to and imports from all regions, except the oil-exporting countries (OPEC), have increased.

The big increase shown here in trade, both exports and imports, is for a group of countries consisting mainly of the East Asian countries other than Japan—China, South Korea, Taiwan, Hong Kong, and Singapore. These economies have grown especially fast, and in the case of China, there has been a considerable reduction of barriers to trade. (They are called "other" in the chart.)

Much attention is always focused on trade with Japan. But Japan is not a particularly large trading partner on either the import or the export side. What stands out in the relation with Japan is the large excess of imports from Japan over exports there.

An excess of total international payments over receipts is not a sign of a problem. That is even more obviously true for an excess of payments to a particular country. The dollars that a country—say, Japan—earns in transactions with the United States, if they are not invested in the United States, will be paid to another country that will use them either to buy goods and services here or to invest here.

The figures in the accompanying charts have been adjusted to constant 1987 dollars, by use of a general price index, to give an approximation to the size of the real increases. But they are not adjusted for changes in the relative prices of goods traded with different regions. Thus the changes shown reflect changes in both the real volumes of goods traded and the prices of the goods involved relative to the general price level. For example, trade with the OPEC countries is shown to decline, not because the number of barrels of oil imported declined but because the price of oil fell relative to the general price level between 1975 and 1993.

EXPORTS BY DESTINATION, 1975 AND 1993

MILLIONS OF $1987

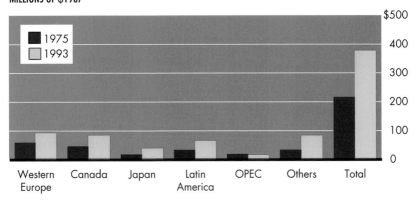

IMPORTS BY SOURCE, 1975 AND 1993

MILLIONS OF $1987

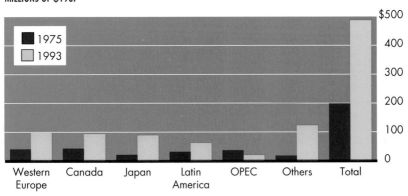

EXCESS OF IMPORTS OVER EXPORTS, 1975 AND 1993

MILLIONS OF $1987

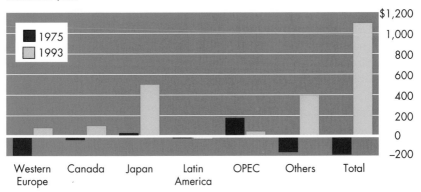

Net American payments to foreigners for imports and other purposes are equal to net investment by foreigners in the United States.

When Americans buy more from the rest of the world than they sell abroad and when the U.S. government or private Americans make payments to foreigners, the foreigners acquire dollars. They can keep the dollars in American banks, or they can invest them in other kinds of investments in this country, such as government securities, American stocks or bonds, American real estate, or American businesses. An individual foreigner can exchange his dollars for some other kind of asset—an asset that is not an investment in the United States. But if he does that, another foreigner is then holding the dollars. If the dollars are not used to buy goods and services from the United States or to make gifts to Americans, the rest of the world can do nothing with them except to invest them here.

The same process works in reverse if the United States is a net earner of foreign currency. The Americans can do nothing with them but invest them abroad.

In 1980 the foreign receipts of Americans from export of goods and services and from earnings on foreign investment exceeded American payments to foreigners by $11.5 billion. That amount was invested by Americans abroad.

By 1993 the situation had changed dramatically. Americans paid $724 billion to foreigners for the purchase of goods and services, and foreigners earned $132 billion from their investments here. Also, Americans, mainly the U.S. government, gave $32 billion to foreign individuals and governments. While foreigners received $888 billion from these transactions, they paid $659 billion for the purchase of goods and services from us and $137 billion for the foreign earnings of Americans. The remainder, $92 billion, they invested in the United States.

The chart at the bottom of the facing page shows the great variation in the size of this capital inflow during the 1980s and early 1990s. The reasons for these variations are discussed on the following pages.

U.S. BALANCE OF PAYMENTS, 1980 AND 1993

BILLIONS OF $

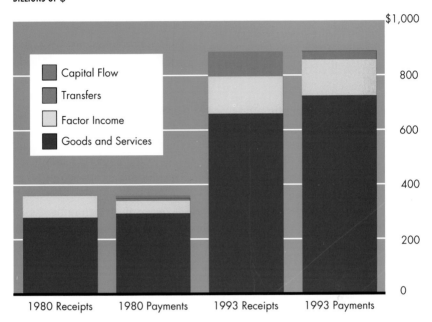

CAPITAL INFLOW TO THE UNITED STATES, 1946–1993

BILLIONS OF $

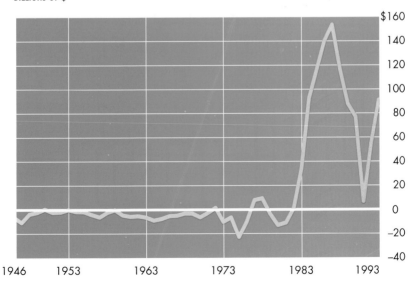

The dollar exchange rate
rose sharply in the early
1980s and subsequently
fell back to about the
level of the 1970s.

The dollar exchange rate is the price of a dollar in a specified foreign currency. Thus in 1993, on the average, the yen exchange rate was 111.08, meaning that the price of a dollar was 111.08 yen.

Exchange rates, like other prices, are determined in markets, by the supply and demand for the things that are to be exchanged. When the quantity of dollars that people want to sell at the existing exchange rate exceeds the quantity that people want to buy, the exchange rate of the dollar falls.

The exchange rate is an important factor in determining the competitiveness of the products of different countries. The higher the dollar is the more expensive U.S. products are for foreigners and the less of them they will buy.

Between 1978 and 1985 the dollar rose relative to the yen by 13.3 percent, from 210 yen to the dollar to 238, as shown in the chart. (The yen is used as an illustration because its movement has been most dramatic, not because it is the most important currency for the United States.) That increased the competitiveness of Japanese products relative to U.S. products. In the same period the U.S. price level (CPI) rose by 65 percent, whereas the Japanese rose by 28 percent. That is a crude measure of what happened to the relative costs of U.S. and Japanese products in their home markets. When these two factors—the exchange rate and the price levels—are combined, the amount of Japanese product that could be obtained for a dollar relative to the amount of U.S. product rose by 46 percent. That is a measure of the change in the "real" exchange rate.

Between 1985 and 1993 the movement was reversed. In 1993 the real dollar exchange rate relative to the yen was 20 percent lower than it had been in 1978.

The bottom chart shows an average of real exchange rates for the countries with which the United States trades. (The average is calculated by weighting each foreign currency by the volume of trade of each country with the United States.) Between 1978 and 1985 this average rose by 57 percent. Between 1985 and 1993 it fell by 32 percent.

YEN PER DOLLAR, 1978–1993

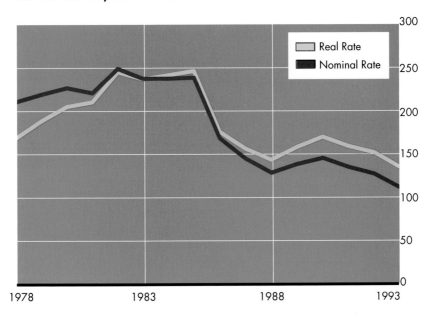

THE REAL VALUE OF THE DOLLAR
RELATIVE TO FOREIGN CURRENCIES, 1978–1993

INDEX: 1973=100

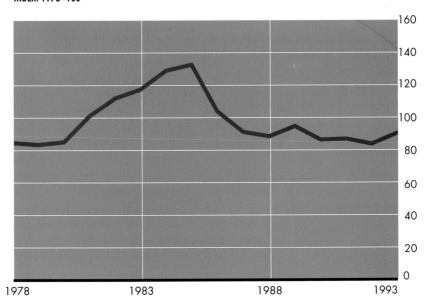

The main factors in the fluctuations of the U.S. foreign balance and exchange rate since the early 1980s have been changes in the attractiveness of investment here and in the cyclical position of the economy.

Beginning in 1981, the attractiveness of net investment in the United States increased greatly. This was partly owing to the increase in the federal deficit, which increased interest rates here relative to interest rates abroad, and perhaps partly owing to tax changes that favored investment here. At the same time the Japanese government relaxed restrictions on the outflow of capital, which permitted more Japanese investment in the United States. Economic difficulties in Latin America discouraged investment there by Americans and others. The combination of these factors concentrated the world's investment on the United States. That raised the exchange rate of the dollar, causing the big increase in the trade deficit that was necessary to balance the capital inflow. A partial indication of the relative attractiveness of investment in the United States is given by the relative movements of interest rates in the United States and Germany, as shown in the chart.

Subsequently this drive to invest in the United States abated. U.S. budget deficits declined as a fraction of GDP. The end of the cold war and the reunification of Germany increased the demand for capital in Europe. Many investors may have felt that they had sufficiently increased the proportion of U.S. dollar assets in their portfolios. The dollar declined, and with it so did the trade deficit.

After 1991 the trade deficit and capital inflows rose again, but the driving force was different from what it had been early in the 1980s. Especially in 1993 and 1994, the U.S. economy was recovering more rapidly than were the economies of Europe and Japan. The U.S. recovery drew more imports into the United States, while exports to the sluggish foreign economies languished. This time there was no strong move to more private foreign investment in the United States. The dollar declined. It did not, however, decline enough to eliminate the trade deficit. That was partly because foreign central banks increased their holdings of dollars, thus supplying the foreign capital inflow needed to balance the trade deficit.

EXCESS OF U.S. INTEREST RATE OVER GERMAN INTEREST RATE, 1980–1994

SHORT-TERM, ADJUSTED FOR INFLATION, PERCENTAGE POINTS

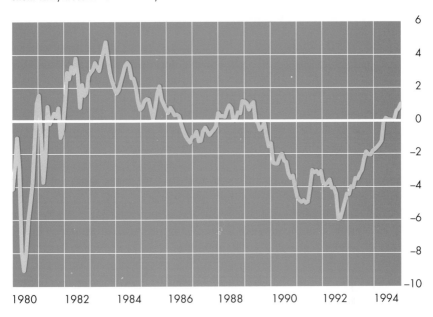

RATIO OF FOREIGN TO U.S. REAL GDP, 1980–1994

INDEX: 1986=100

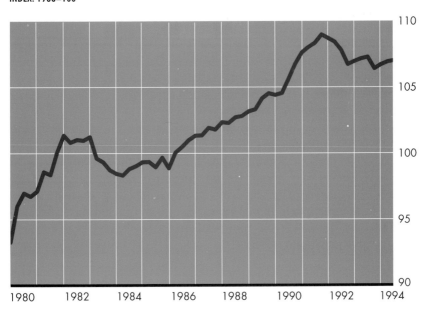

Concern about the United States having become a "net debtor" to the rest of the world is unfounded, because the condition is not a threat to the United States or a sign of economic weakness.

As the United States imported capital during the 1980s, and as foreign ownership of U.S. government securities and some U.S. private assets, like Radio City, became more obvious, many people expressed fear that the United States was becoming a net debtor. They meant that the U.S. assets owned by foreigners were coming to exceed the foreign assets owned by Americans.

The net foreign debt, however, is only a statistical aggregate without any economic significance—only a comparison of arbitrarily chosen totals of assets and liabilities. It does not measure the net worth, net income, or net cash flow of any individual, association, or country.

Some economic significance attaches to the measurement of the net amount of productive wealth owned by Americans, as a source of the income of Americans. For this purpose it is necessary to compare the total amount of wealth owned by Americans—not just the wealth they own abroad—with their liabilities to the rest of the world. Despite the increase in American wealth owned by foreigners, the total amount of wealth owned at home and abroad by Americans increased during the 1980s.

Sometimes people worry about what would happen if foreigners wanted to take home their American assets. Of course, most of the assets they have here—Radio City, for example—they could not literally take home. But they could, in principle, sell their assets for dollars and then convert their dollars into other currencies.

The ability of the United States to meet such an unlikely development would not depend in the amount of foreign assets owned by Americans but on the total wealth and productivity of the United States. The dollar exchange rate would decline, and the United States would sell more goods abroad. The only way that foreigners as a whole can "take back" their investments in the United States is by purchasing more goods and services from us, just as they acquired their investments here by selling us more goods and services.

U.S. ASSETS AND FOREIGN OWNERSHIP, 1982–1993

TRILLIONS OF $

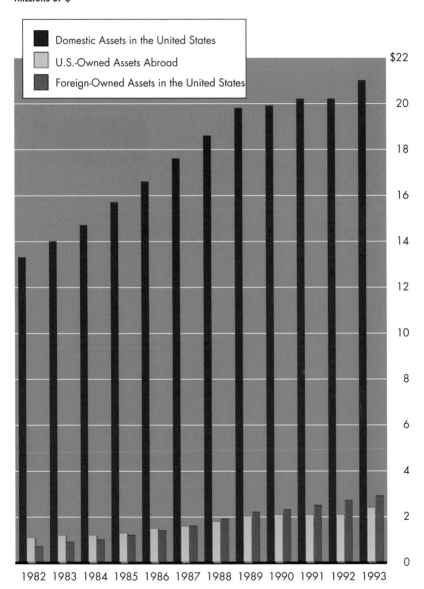

Domestic Assets in the United States

U.S.-Owned Assets Abroad

Foreign-Owned Assets in the United States

$22

20

18

16

14

12

10

8

6

4

2

0

1982 1983 1984 1985 1986 1987 1988 1989 1990 1991 1992 1993

SOURCES

Page	Source		Page	Source		Page	Source
Part One	5	A, D	Part Eight	109	C	Part Thirteen	203	D
	7	U		111	W		205	D
	9	P, U		113	E		207	S
	11	Z		115	Y		209	S
	13	D		117	E		211	D
Part Two	17	D		119	T		213	C
	19	D		121	D		215	O
	21	D		123	D, AA		217	J
	23	D, AA	Part Nine	127	V		219	S
Part Three	27	D		129	E		221	K
	29	D		131	E		223	U
	31	D		133	E		225	S
	33	D		135	E		227	S
Part Four	37	D		137	Q		229	C
	39	D	Part Ten	141	E, X		231	S
	41	D		143	E	Part Fourteen	235	H
	43	D		145	D		237	D
	45	B, D		147	E, AA		239	H, D
	47	D		149	D		241	C, AA
	49	D		151	J		243	E
Part Five	53	J	Part Eleven	155	B	Part Fifteen	247	D
	55	E, F, AA		157	B		249	E, G
	57	J		159	B, D, AA		251	D, M
	59	D		161	B, D, AA		253	L
	61	D		163	B	Part Sixteen	257	D
	63	D		165	E		259	D
	65	D	Part Twelve	169	D		261	D
	67	D, J		171	D		263	D
	69	D		173	J, R		265	B
	71	D		175	N		267	B
	73	D		177	J		269	D
	75	U		179	J			
	77	J		181	J			
	79	J		183	J, AA			
Part Six	83	J		185	J			
	85	D		187	J			
	87	J		189	J			
	89	J		191	J			
	91	D, J, AA		193	J			
	93	I, J, AA		195	N, B, J			
	95	J		197	B, J			
Part Seven	99	D, J, AA		199	B			
	101	D, J, AA						
	103	D, J, AA						
	105	C, E, AA						

References

A. Balke, N. S., and R. J. Gordon, "The Estimation of Prewar Gross National Product: Methodology and New Evidence," *Journal of Political Economy*, vol. 97.

B. Board of Governors of the Federal Reserve System.

C. Congressional Budget Office.

D. Department of Commerce, Bureau of Economic Analysis.

E. Department of Commerce, Bureau of the Census.

F. Department of Education, National Center for Education Statistics.

G. Department of Energy, Energy Information Administration.

H. Department of Health and Human Services, Health Care Financing Administration.

I. Department of Health and Human Services, National Center for Health Statistics.

J. Department of Labor, Bureau of Labor Statistics.

K. Department of the Treasury, Office of Tax Analysis.

L. Eisner, Robert, *The Total Incomes System of Accounts* (Chicago: University of Chicago Press, 1989).

M. Environmental Protection Agency.

N. Friedman, Milton, and Anna J. Schwartz, *Monetary Trends in the United States and the United Kingdom* (Chicago: University of Chicago Press, 1982).

O. Kollmann, Geoffrey, "Social Security: The Relationship of Taxes and Benefits for Past, Present, and Future Retirees," Congressional Research Service, 1993.

P. Maddison, Angus, *The World Economy in the Twentieth Century*, 1989.

Q. Mincey, Ronald B., and Susan J. Wiener, "The Under Class in the 1980s: Changing Concept, Constant Reality," Urban Institute, 1993.

R. Moore, Geoffrey H., ed., *Business Cycle Indicators, Basic Data on Cyclical Indicators*, vol. II (Princeton: Princeton University Press, 1961).

S. Office of Management and Budget.

(continues)

T. O'Neill, June, and Solomon Polacheck, "Why the Gender Gap in Wages Narrowed in the 1980s," *Journal of Labor Economics*, 1993, vol. 11, pt. 1; O'Neill, June, "The Causes and Significance of the Declining Gender Gap," mimeo, 1994.

U. Organization for Economic Cooperation and Development.

V. Ruggles, P., *Drawing the Line: Alternative Poverty Measures and Their Implications for Public Policy*, 1990.

W. Slesnick, Daniel T., "Consumption, Needs, and Inequality," *International Economic Review*, vol. 35, August 1994.

X. Small Business Administration.

Y. Smith, J. P., and F. R. Welch, "Black Economic Progress after Myrdal," *Journal of Economic Literature*, June 1989, and calculations of J. P. Smith.

Z. World Bank.

AA. Authors' calculations.

ABOUT THE AUTHORS

Herbert Stein, a senior fellow at the American Enterprise Institute, was a member of the President's Council of Economic Advisers from 1969 to 1971 and was chairman from 1972 to 1974. He has been a consultant to the State Department on the economy of Israel and a member of President Reagan's Economic Policy Advisory Board, and he is the A. Willis Robertson Professor of Economics Emeritus at the University of Virginia. In addition, Mr. Stein is a member of the Board of Contributors of the *Wall Street Journal.*

He earned his Ph.D. in economics from the University of Chicago. In 1989 he received the Frank E. Seidman Award in Political Economy. Among his recent books are *On the Other Hand...Essays on Economics, Economists, and Politics* (AEI, 1995); *Presidential Economics: The Making of Economic Policy from Roosevelt to Clinton* (AEI, rev. ed. 1994); *The Fiscal Revolution in America* (AEI, rev. ed. 1990); and *Washington Bedtime Stories* (1986).

Murray Foss, a visiting scholar at the American Enterprise Institute, was a senior research associate at the National Bureau of Economic Research from 1975 to 1978 and was a senior staff economist in charge of forecasting at the Council of Economic Advisers from 1970 to 1975. He served as editor of the *Survey of Current Business* and as chief of the Current Business Analysis Division of the Bureau of Economic Analysis of the Department of Commerce.

Mr. Foss is the author of *Changes in the Workweek of Fixed Capital: U.S. Manufacturing, 1929–1976* (AEI, 1981) and *Changing Utilization of Fixed Capital: An Element in Long-Term Growth* (AEI, 1984). He edited a National Bureau of Economic Research conference volume, *The U.S. National Income and Product Accounts* (1983), and was coeditor of the conference volume *Price Measurements and Their Uses* (1993).

A NOTE ON THE BOOK

This book was edited by Cheryl Weissman, of the AEI Press. Allyson Brown, graphic desinger of AEI, designed the book and drew the charts. The text was set in Century and Futura. Publication Technology Corporation, of Fairfax, Virginia, set the type and produced the film from which the book was printed.

The AEI Press is the publisher for the American Enterprise Institute for Public Policy Research, 1150 17th Street, N.W., Washington, D.C. 20036: *Christopher C. DeMuth*, publisher; *Dana Lane*, Director; *Ann Petty*, editor; *Cheryl Weissman*, editor; *Leigh Tripoli*, editor; *Lisa Roman*, editorial assistant (rights and permissions).